Jesus and the Quest
for
Secular Justice

Jesus and the Quest
for
Secular Justice

Pierre L'Abbé

Seraphim Editions

The publisher gratefully acknowledges the financial assistance of the Canada Council for the Arts.

The Canada Council for the Arts
Le Conseil des Arts du Canada

Published in 2005 by
Seraphim Editions
238 Emerald St. N.
Hamilton, ON
Canada L8L 5K8

Library and Archives Canada Cataloguing in Publication

L'Abbé, Pierre, 1959-
Jesus and the quest for secular justice / Pierre L'Abbé ; edited by Gilles M. Mongeau.

ISBN 0-9735487-2-X

1. Jesus Christ—In literature. 2. Secularism. I. Mongeau, Gilles M. (Gilles Michel-Joseph), 1964- II. Title.

BT303.L32 2005232   C2005-900932-2

Cover: Salvador Dalí, *Christ of St. John of the Cross,* © Glasgow Museums: St. Mungo's Museum of Religious Life and Art
Author's photo: Liz Szynkowski
Designed by Perkolator {Kommunikation}

Printed and bound in Canada

CONTENTS

Preface / 7

5

PREFACE

THE IDEA FOR this book first began to take shape when I was approached by a woman at a reception who asked to speak to me in confidence. Her daughter had joined a cult and she thought that I, a student of religion, could explain why. The woman was extremely perplexed because, in her words, she had raised her daughter without any "religious prejudice" in an "atheistic household." So it did not make sense that her bookish seventeen-year-old would search for religion and subsequently take up with a cult.

From what I could tell, the girl had not taken up with a cult at all, but a Christian group with social activist leanings. I listened patiently to the mother, but ultimately had no wisdom to offer. What I wanted to tell her was that her daughter had turned to religion because people are religious by nature, but this went against what I had been taught. I did feel that surely I should be able to turn to my education for an answer to what seemed like a simple question.

When I think of where my inhibition came from, I recall meeting two good friends the week we began our doctorates. When we talked about why we were there, one of them said it was because he was fascinated with the universality of religious belief. I had to agree, but had a feeling that this was not something I should admit. In academic schools of religion one finds a view borrowed from the social sciences that religion is a social construct; that it is a societal response to comprehending or coping with one's environment. In these schools, most adhere to or pay lip-service to this view.

It was my own discomfort in thinking I should not agree with my friend, and my discomfort in hesitating to offer an answer to a woman—bewildered with her daughter's behaviour—that made me see that many questions people were asking about religion were not being answered. So I resolved to try to write a book for those people who feel they have a foot in both worlds, the religious and the secular.

Over the years, as people have asked me questions about religion, I have turned to my education for answers but I have always seemed to come up short. The academic study of religion has been asking a different set of questions than the questions put to me by people I have come across in everyday life. At the risk of oversimplifying things, I would say that academics have been concerned with understanding religions, while many of the people who have asked me about religion have been trying to understand themselves.

To get a handle on what it was that perplexed people so much about religion, I began to see that most questions fell into three groups. The first concerned Jesus Christ, and in particular, things people heard in the media about the historical Jesus related to the Dead Sea Scrolls, or the Jesus Seminar. Media reports had put so much in question about Jesus that people were wondering whether there was any evidence at all to support the existence of an historical figure called Jesus of Nazareth.

A second group of questions concerned the endurance of religion and faith. It almost appeared to me as though people were asking if they should get on the bandwagon and leave what remnants of faith they had behind, since fifty years hence the established churches would have ceased to exist.

8

A third group of questions surrounded morality. I got the sense that people were obsessed with issues of right and wrong. Not on a personal level but on a grander eternal or cosmic level. They were obsessed with the possibility of a moral world and the possibility of a final sense of justice. All religions have placed morality and good conduct within a larger religious context. All of the major world religions, I believe, see their role as guiding people towards a final end or salvation. Morality plays an important part in this, but it is often not a guiding or central role. From the people I have heard asking questions, however, I have been left with the impression that they see morality and religion as more integrally bound. They are searching for answers about the link between moral behaviour and an eternal destiny, and they expect religions to come up with credible answers to their questions about an eternal and final justice.

A number of years ago, I had the opportunity to discuss with the publisher of Seraphim Editions, Maureen Whyte, some of the questions which occupied me on the relevance of Jesus to contemporary society. She too felt that there were questions particularly surrounding the life of the historical Jesus which contemporary society needed to address. Out of our conversation came the framework for this book.

In researching and writing, my ideas have evolved somewhat. Many of the thinkers of the past have tended to approach these questions from either a religious or a secular point of view with arguments or solutions presented in terms of contrasting worldviews. I began to see the society that was generating the questions as having a different structure than what previous writers had seen. It became evident to me that most people were operating in a dual culture, both religious and secular, and carrying on a cultural dialogue. One conclusion I drew was that the secularist's argument that religious views and explanations are those of the past is itself an argument of the past. Freud, Marx and Darwin all thought that Jesus would be dead by the advent of the third millennium, hardly entering into a new and vigorous period of his life as seems to be the case in most parts of the world. If Christianity is to be judged by any historical or objective standard, then not only is it alive, it is doing well. In fact, Buddhist, Hindu, and Islamic religious expressions are all very much alive and far from facing extinction.

Virtually all Christians today have doubts about the veracity of the biblical accounts of the life of Jesus: many through reports of biblical research and through our own critical examination of the biblical accounts based on what we know to be true of the natural world. What is difficult to accept is that this has been the experience of virtually all Christians from the time the Gospels were recorded. Many Christians feel they would like to move toward a sense of greater conviction in their beliefs or to move toward a discerning rationalism. Nevertheless, we, as Christians, go on functioning in our daily lives with a critical approach to our personal beliefs and religion as a whole. Some of us go on partially believing the biblical accounts of the life of Jesus, and some, not believing them at all, finding instead ways to direct our need for spiritual expression to a higher, more impersonal divinity. We simply go on with our doubts. We populate an age of critical believers.

Finally, I would like to express my gratitude to Gilles Mongeau and Allan Briesmaster for their candid and meticulous criticism and many helpful editorial suggestions. However, the ideas expressed here and responsibility for the final form of the arguments made remain solely my own.

1

THE HISTORICAL JESUS

The Perpetual Fascination with the Historical Jesus

A S A STUDENT at McGill I restocked the shelves of the
Faculty of Religious Studies library. After a few weeks,
this job took me down into the lower basement, which
housed the "old and seldom used" volumes. When I rolled back
the fire-door, I experienced an epiphany of a sort, which in
retrospect I can only describe as a historiographical epiphany:
one that completely changed how I thought about the past and
about "doing history." I had lived with a comfortable sense of
reassurance that ours was an age of knowledge and critical
inquiry and that, with the exception of a few "high" cultures, to
move back into the past was to move into periods of diminish-
ing collective knowledge when people were less critical.
Standing there in the basement, as I flipped on the lights, I saw
aisle after aisle of bookshelves become illuminated. Far from
finding the small and prized holdings I expected, these stacks
were vast, larger even than the main collection where students
and professors often shuffled shoulder to shoulder down the
aisles. As I began to wander through, I saw that these stacks were
filled with books from before the turn of the 20th century, and
although I knew that scholars in the 19th century had been
active on the subject of religion, it was astonishing to think that
the number of volumes produced in that century could have

rivalled the number produced in my own. What struck me most was finding so many volumes on the historical personage and nature of Jesus. Blowing the dust from the faded spines, I read titles like *Jesus of Nazareth: Embracing a Sketch of Jewish History to the Time of His Birth*, *The Historical Jesus and Mythical Christ*, and *The Life of Jesus Christ in its Historical Connexion and Historical Development*. These titles made me wonder how contemporary books on Jesus could assert his humanity as a burning issue which scholars were only recently bringing to light. Suddenly, I understood that to bring home the message that Jesus was in fact just a man carried the same cachet in 1980 as it did in 1880.

Taken by themselves, books written since the mid-19th century that treat Jesus as an historical personage would make him the most written-about figure in history. The fascination with the life of Jesus has spawned whole areas of scholarly enquiry, from biblical archaeology, through Roman imperial administration, to first-century Jewish religious practice. The nature of critical scholarly work on Jesus has become unique in the field of historical research. Since the latter half of the 20th century it has come to rely heavily on sources from associated movements and cultures: texts which did not make it into the accepted Christian canon,[1] the Nag Hammadi texts, the Dead Sea Scrolls, and especially Gnostic literature.[2] Increasingly, scholars have also turned to textual and archaeological evidence from neighbouring cultures and times.

Like many others, I have read with fascination the books that have shed new light on Jesus' society. Recent scholarship has been able to extract considerable new knowledge from the diverse set of cultures in the middle-eastern world in the centuries immediately preceding and following the time of Jesus. Yet, it is true that scholarship that has become this expansive would not be considered acceptable in most fields of historical

research. This has led to a level of conjecture not found elsewhere, and brought about the tricky situation in which it has
become difficult to tell how applicable such exploratory
research is to the task of shedding new light on the life of
Jesus or his times. Nevertheless, scholars find themselves in a
challenging position because of the wealth of literature on the
historical Jesus. Expectations are very high, requiring scholars
to probe sources ever more closely and to extract novel conclusions and interpretations.

The Jesus Seminar

IN RECENT YEARS, many books on the historical Jesus have
been associated with a project known as the Jesus Seminar.
The Seminar itself has gained considerable notoriety because
of its controversial method of voting with red, pink or black
dice to establish the historical veracity of the sayings and deeds
of Jesus. This practice immediately raised suspicions among
the public and scholars alike, who take it for granted that
democracy and scholarship do not mix. More importantly, I
think, the Seminar has gained attention because in the public
imagination there is an unease with accepting the truth of all
the Gospels' recorded sayings of Jesus, and so people are anxious
to hear what conclusions would be arrived at by a group of
eminent scholars who have spent their lives studying these sayings. At the same time, this dry forum for deciding on the
"red letterness" of Jesus' words has also given people a strange
comfort, because we have been so disposed to accepting or
not accepting the "Truth" of the Gospel, that in the public
imagination, to doubt some sayings of Jesus was to doubt the
Gospel record altogether; and here was a group of scholars

asserting in a detached way that "some of this is definitely true." If this were the case, then everyone could participate in the process either vicariously, by following the voting, or by leafing through the Gospel pages themselves and casting their own vote on each saying.

The Tradition of Critical Scholarship

A NUMBER OF significant works on the life of Jesus have appeared in recent years. Particularly influential has been John Dominic Crossan's *The Historical Jesus,*[3] which demonstrates the influence of the Greek tradition of the Cynics on the life of a Jesus tied to a subservient peasant class in Galilee under Roman domination. Also of note is John Meier's *A Marginal Jew: Rethinking the Historical Jesus,* and the work of Burton Mack, which provides an impressive analysis of the life of Jesus based on the missing "Q" texts, believed to be the source of the synoptic Gospels.[4]

These scholars are very much aware of the long tradition of critical scholarship, of which they are a part, and try to build on the work of earlier writers who, like them, have attempted to offer an accurate portrait of Jesus' historical setting and his activities. They have tried, in part, to accomplish this by returning directly to Jesus' Palestine without seeing it through the overlay of the thought and early doctrinal formulations of ecclesiastical organizations of the first, second and third centuries. As these writers suggest, it is this ecclesiastical framework which forms the basis of the doctrinal conceptions of Jesus currently held by all major Christian denominations, including the mainline Protestant Churches, Catholicism, and Orthodoxy.

The first important writer to whom contemporary scholars

usually point as exemplifying this orientation is David Friedrich Strauss. As a young man in 1835, he wrote *The Life of Jesus Critically Examined*. Since that time, Strauss' stated mission of de-mythologizing has been picked up in hundreds of works that have attempted to critically examine various aspects of Jesus' life as portrayed in the Gospel accounts. These writers suggest that further explication of first century trends in the society in Palestine, such as the prevalence of "wonder workers" or the activities of "nationalist zealots," can explain what the motivations of Jesus really were and account for the climax of his life in a confrontation with Roman and/or Hebrew authorities.

On the one hand, so many of these accounts exist that one has to question how scholars could justify returning to the same topics while offering only marginally differing treatments. There is no parallel in other areas of historical research. But on the other hand, it is also the responsibility of the scholar to provide the best possible account of the latest research and do so with an analysis that responds to the questions currently being asked by the public, students, and the larger academic community.

Ernest Renan (1823-1892)

ERNEST RENAN WAS the first scholar to have a major international impact and whose influence was to stretch far beyond the scholarly community and affect how the public at large regarded the nature and personage of Jesus of Nazareth. A French scholar of wide-ranging gifts and interests, Renan was well-known in his country, where he was in the vanguard of introducing secular culture and understanding not only to the academic community but also to the French intelligentsia and into political circles. His *Life of Jesus*[5] was widely translated through the latter decades of the 19th century. Its influence was remarkable in the English-speaking world, in both Britain and the United States, where it went into multiple printings in the first few years of its appearance.

Renan's position was that Jesus of Nazareth was not a divine person; yet he posited that Jesus was, nonetheless, a type of super-ethical being, completely human, but beyond our normal understanding of a person's ethical or humanist capabilities. Many criticised Renan, and pegged his Jesus as a quasi-divinity and thus accused him of wanting to have the best of both worlds. Religious thinkers saw this figure as neither divine nor inspired, while secularist thinkers saw him as nothing but a popular writer's attempt to pander to the public's appetite for intellectual compromise. Despite all the criticism and his ability to satisfy neither camp, Renan's book remained remarkably popular with the general public, who were looking for a figure to respond to their insecurities. They could appeal to such a figure for consolation, and at the same time, he did not offend their sense of reality. Nestled in a century of recurring revolutions and counter-revolutions, freethinking anti-clericals and reactionary nationalists, these people were trying to grapple, as we are today, with the understanding that there is simply a contradiction between what we know, and want, of Jesus.

Henri Barbusse (1873-1935)

YET ANOTHER EXAMPLE of a popular work which asserts the humanity of Jesus of Nazareth is Henri Barbusse's *Jésus*.[6] Barbusse was a French communist active in the 1920's and 30's, best known as a writer of novels of austere and shocking realism. He often treated religious themes and ideas that allowed people to confront their own humanist reality. His most popular novel, *L'enfer (Hell)*, allows a man to look, through a crude and voyeuristic setting, into the lives of other persons in their most debased, raw state. Although this work is on the surface devoid of any sense of hope or push toward the betterment of human society, it is intended to confront people with just that: the point at which they have to move forward. It presents a type of humanist's creed, that only by working together can we achieve a better world. This truly reflects Barbusse's life's work as a communist. He held strongly to the belief that through political and collective action we could not just temporarily better the lot of human beings, but permanently "raise the bar" on the state of human relations. Barbusse's Jesus is not semi-divine like Renan's; he is, strictly speaking, a human figure but also encapsulates that humanist hope Barbusse carried as a communist. It is Jesus' ability to carry forward the hope of a world transformed that makes him attractive to Barbusse.

Barbusse was also prescient in his use of sources, foreshadowing the type of scholarship that would come to be employed by scholars in the late 20th century in their search for authorities outside the canon. Barbusse turned to the Apocrypha, Gnostic writings extant at that time, and other "extra"-canonical works, to put forward the claim that only with the addition of these other "suppressed" writings could a true picture of Jesus be developed.

As with other scholars today, in Barbusse we find a bias toward presenting these "other" works as "truer" sources, even though they post-date the canonical books of the Christian scriptures and significantly post-date the letters of Paul and the synoptic Gospels. In some cases, scholars argue for the validity of these other "extra"-canonical books on the basis that they have earlier oral or written sources within them, that can be carved out in order to create a truer picture of Jesus of Nazareth and the early Christians. While this may in some cases be a necessary and often fruitful exercise, the end result is that a later work is given precedence over an earlier work.

Critical Scholarship and Claims to Truth

CRITICAL SCHOLARS IN our own time, like popular writers such as Barbusse and Renan, have tried to give us an alternative picture of Jesus of Nazareth. Collectively, their methods are informed by the desire to reshape the picture of who Jesus was and the picture of who he should be in the contemporary imagination. Virtually all of these scholars assert a position of authority according to which they suggest that their picture of Jesus is an accurate one: a picture brought together piecemeal by new and insightful scholarship and a more reliable return to the sources.[7]

Strangely enough, this type of forceful assertion of validity is something we have come to associate not with scholars at all, but with Churches. Churches taking religious positions, positions based on precepts of faith or their views and judgements on what they regard to be true, such as in creeds or bodies of doctrine. The public at large regards these Churches, when functioning in their proper roles, as bodies that assert positions based on their own principles.

All of the major Churches, for the past fifty years, have been trying to disassociate their "Truth" from scientific or literal truth. The only noteworthy exceptions are the evangelical Churches that continue to promote the identification of scientific truth with a literal reading of the biblical books. What makes this an issue that will never go away is the desire for a resolution of the tension people inherently feel between the truth of a spiritual reality they believe or would like to believe in, and the experience of the empirical world in their daily lives.

At its most basic level, this is an experience of reason. In virtually every moment of our conscious lives, we have to apply what we understand to be rules of logic and consistency, simply to continue to exist as human beings. When we turn to considering larger, or metaphysical questions, such as *Where do we come from?* and *Why are we here?* reason seems to be able to posit explanations for existence which are inconsistent with what we know of the empirical world. Many of us are acquainted with Aristotelian or other philosophies which arrive at a fundamental unity between rational inquiry and the belief in spiritual realities.

At a second level, the experience of the tension between the empirical world and the truth of spiritual realities is one of scientific enquiry. Here, rules of logic and consistency are laid out in a framework of experimentation and hypothesis. Many who argue for the acceptance of a belief in spiritual reality have been heartened by developments in scientific enquiry in the later 20th century, particularly in the areas of atomic physics and cosmology. Here, the development of the relativity, quantum and chaos theories has seriously compromised theories of determinism and related conceptions of an ordered universe.

At a third level, the tension between the experience of the empirical world and the truth of spiritual realities is one of determinism, the belief that everything has a natural cause. We are subject to a determinism based on empirical realities that we experience in our immediate environment. It is this experience, of our immediate environment, I think, with its apparent adherence to simple laws of nature, and logical consequence, which makes the tension between the truth of spiritual realties and our experience of the empirical world a perennial issue.

The Spectrum of Approaches to the Life of Jesus

NO MATTER HOW guarded their words, writers such as Barbusse and Crossan are creating their own quasi-doctrinal positions by re-sorting and re-valuing their primary sources. Albert Schweitzer, in his book *The Quest for the Historical Jesus*,[8] chronicled the abundance of books like theirs, each making its case for who Jesus really was, each attempting to refashion Jesus in its own image. This is, of course, not uncommon within religious groups, particularly new splinter religious groups that seek to recreate the Messiah in their own image: firstly by attempting to discredit other interpretations of the Messiah and then by re-sorting and sifting the canonical authorities.

The tenacity with which some scholars, associated with the Jesus Seminar, have asserted their own hegemony has allowed them to conclude that views they consider less scholarly than their own are conservative. In these circles, "conservative" has become a polite, but pejorative, euphemism for faith-laden. The acceptance of this view has become widespread and has

20

led to some curious outcomes. One case in point being the biblical scholar Thomas Wright, who, bearing the label conservative, has entered into a written debate with Marcus Borg, a scholar associated with the Jesus Seminar.[9] Together they set out their views – the supposed scholarly scientific liberal view as opposed to a Church-based faith-laden "conservative view" – in the book *The Meaning of Jesus: two visions*. When we take into account the total spectrum of the approaches to the life of Jesus, or the historical Jesus, or the accuracy of Bible, then the position in which Wright has allowed himself to be placed seems particularly bizarre.

I would like to outline eight positions which I think typify approaches to the life of Jesus. These positions represent the full range of people who write on Jesus in terms of his humanity and divinity and of approaches to a literal reading of the Bible and biblical inerrancy.

Eight Approaches

THE FIRST APPROACH would be that of an ideological fundamentalism. People in this camp typically choose a hodgepodge of texts, which taken collectively, can only serve to justify their own ideological positions. In short, the approach taken to the historical Jesus is one which is self-generated. Although it uses biblical texts, because of its free hand in picking and choosing and interpreting at will, it has derived a view to justify its social, cultural or fundamentalist stance. Representative of this approach would be so-called "TV Evangelism" and fundamentalist groups with right-wing political affinities.

The second approach would be of those who advocate a literal reading of the Bible, often thought of as fundamentalist.

The important issue for this group is that they maintain the integrity of the biblical text. They hold to biblical inerrancy: the conviction, not only that the Bible cannot be wrong, but also that it is literally true. But unlike proponents of the first approach, they would be concerned with providing explanations for "apparent inconsistencies" in the text. People in this camp may also support creationism. Nevertheless, writers representative of this approach function co-operatively in the secular world and accept extra-religious (scientific-deterministic) discourse. They would see religious and scientific-deterministic discourses as each operating within their own realms; with the proviso that they would not allow the latter to compromise their approach to biblical inerrancy. Groups with Puritan and Jansenist leanings and evangelicals without strong political ties exemplify this view.

The third approach in the spectrum would be that group of writers which accepts the literal truth of the biblical text, but at the same time also allows that it may contain certain mythic elements. Typical of this approach would be to say that the first eleven chapters of Genesis, from the story of the Garden of Eden through Noah, are mythic, while the literal account would start with Abraham and the lives of the Patriarchs. Also included as mythic by this group would be the more prophetic passages of the Hebrew Scriptures. Literal truth, however, is largely maintained for the entire New Testament, including the accounts of Jesus' resurrection, miracles and appearances. This approach is largely adopted by what we think of today as (theologically) left-wing mainline Protestant Churches, including many of the larger groups, such as Baptists, Presbyterians, etc. This approach also largely typified the Roman Catholic scholarship prior to Vatican II, and still includes a large segment of the Roman Catholic and Orthodox public.

The fourth approach in the spectrum is that which accepts the Truth, with a capital "T," of the text, but questions the whole notion of literal truth. When challenged on the issue of the literal meaning of the text, proponents of this approach often raise philosophical objections to the notion of literal truth, such as how truth is established and our interpretation of what is scientific truth. Furthermore, they question how scientific knowledge was interpreted in the past and how the writers of the biblical text would have approached and understood truth in their own cultural context. For this approach, truth must be sought through a tradition that interprets scripture. Without the tradition of biblical interpretation, a plurality of outcomes becomes inevitable and a tradition is needed to guide biblical understanding. People representative of this position would question the resurrection and resurrection accounts, but not the Truth of the resurrection. Representative of this approach would be much of contemporary Catholicism and theologically right of centre Protestantism (Lutherans, Anglicans), as practiced in the western world.

From the Text to Secular Culture

IN CROSSING THE midline of this spectrum, we pass from approaches for which the Bible is normative, to approaches for which secular culture is normative. On this side of the spectrum, the fifth approach would maintain that the truth is in the message. Here we leave behind any support for a literal reading of the Bible, or the notion that truth is found in what is written. This approach seeks a rapprochement with secular culture. It tends to distil the messages of Jesus and make them compatible with our broader cultural understanding of the 21st century and of deterministic empiricism. Proponents of this approach would hold to ideas such as "the resurrection is within us." Typical representatives of this approach would be the liberal wing of the Anglican Church, and others struggling to find a place for an established Church in contemporary secular society where it could be fully accepted.

The sixth approach in the spectrum would be that group of scholars and people who are embarrassed by the biblical tradition. This group seeks to explain or provide an apology for a literal interpretation of the tradition. It regards secular culture as a higher and "rationalist" culture. It provides no coherent approach to the life of Jesus or the historical Jesus. It hopes to overcome its embarrassment by looking forward to a time when religious people will all have a rationalist outlook and conflict between religious culture and rationalist-secular culture will be minimized. Many Christian churches that have adopted a social activist stance would be among the groups who associate themselves with this approach. It is common within liberal protestant Churches, including the liberal wing of the United Church of Canada.

The seventh position in the spectrum would be the "disinterested" or neutral approach to the historical Jesus. Here the attempt is to find a biblical interpretation which is consistent with scholarship as it is commonly found within the social sciences and humanities. The Bible is studied as an historical text, or more particularly as a "text." It can be valued for its literary merit and for the insights it gives into what may have been happening at the time of Jesus. Issues concerning theology (doctrine) or faith are avoided by writers representing this position, though philosophical reflections are acceptable. This is an attempt at a value-free appraisal of the historical

24

Jesus. It is typified by academics whose specialities lie outside the area of religion.

The eighth and last position in the spectrum is that of the anti-belief approach. Central to this approach is the conviction that faith must be written out of the history of Jesus and out of Christian history. The job of the writer is not only to re-examine the historical sources in a critical fashion but to strip the entire veil of Christian interpretation which has been dropped over these sources, in order to reveal their true historical character. It is only through this stripping-off that a true picture of the historical Jesus can be found. Writers in this group choose their own texts in order to write a new history which they regard as more valid. This group is ideological in that its starting point is that faith has distorted our ability to perceive the historical Jesus. There is an attempt to recreate an historical Jesus in their own image: that is, a Jesus that reflects their own view of what the historical Jesus would be, as they sort, cut, unveil and choose their sources. Typical of this approach would be the scholars associated with the Jesus Seminar.

By following the spectrum through its eight positions and examining the people who are typically associated with each group and their various affiliations, a link becomes evident between the characterization of the life of Jesus of Nazareth and the lives of the proponents who put forward these lives. In short, the life of Jesus is very much the life of the people whose business it is to talk about Jesus.

The Rehabilitation of Jesus

IN MY EXPERIENCE, many people who write about the life of Jesus feel under siege from a larger secular world which purports to maintain a positivistic[10] view of society in which religion is a

DISINTERESTED
- biblical interpretation must be consistent with the methods of the social sciences and humanities
- the bible is a text which can be studied for its historical or literary merit
- issues concerning theology or faith are bracketed out

EXEMPLIFIED BY:
- academics interested in religion, outside of Religious Studies and Theology schools

ANTI-BELIEF
- Christian history is a distortion of history
- only a critical examination of sources can achieve a history of Jesus
- characterized by the creation of new texts
- do not accept theological discourse

EXEMPLIFIED BY:
- Jesus Seminar

MOST IDEOLOGICAL

SECULAR CULTURE

THE TEXT

FUNDAMENTALISM
- ideological
- picking and choosing of texts to support ideology
- theology is self-generated
- characterized by the creation of new texts
- does not accept scientific discourse

EXEMPLIFIED BY:
- "TV Evangelism"
- Fundamentalist groups with right-wing political leanings

BIBLICAL LITERALISM
- often grouped with fundamentalists, but maintain vehemently the integrity of the biblical text
- accepts scientific discourse outside the realm of religion

EXEMPLIFIED BY:
- Evangelical protestants
- Puritans / Jansenists

MESSAGE
▓ truth lies in the message
▓ rejects biblical literalism
▓ attempts a rapprochement
with scientific, rationalist
culture
▓ characterized by distilling
Jesus' message to make it
relevant
EXEMPLIFIED BY:
◆ liberal Anglicans

EMBARRASSED
▓ seeks to provide an apology
for the biblical tradition
▓ regards secular culture as a
higher, rational culture
▓ looks forward to a time
when everyone in the Church
will have a rationalist
approach to the life of Jesus
EXEMPLIFIED BY:
◆ Liberal wing of the United
Church of Canada
◆ Christian social activists

LEAST IDEOLOGICAL

IS NORMATIVE
────────────────────────
IS NORMATIVE

TRUTH
▓ questions the notion of
literal truth and scientific
truth
▓ asserts that texts must be
read in the historical contexts
of their writers
▓ truth must be sought with
help of a tradition
EXEMPLIFIED BY:
◆ contemporary western
Catholicism
◆ right of centre major
protestant Churches,
Lutherans, Anglicans

QUALIFIED LITERALISM
▓ accepts the literal truth of
New Testament but holds to
mythic elements in the
Hebrew Scriptures
EXEMPLIFIED BY:
◆ Roman Catholic theology
before Vatican II
◆ major (theologically) left
protestant Churches,
Presbyterians, Baptists

recalcitrant element that people will in time outgrow. Although the once-influential theories of Darwin, Marx, Freud, Comte, and Durkheim are regarded as somewhat outmoded in their claims that religion will be superseded, nevertheless there is a lingering feeling amongst these writers that the relevance of their subject matter is being questioned, not only by the academic community, but by society as a whole.

This sense of being judged has had a direct effect on writings on the historical Jesus and presentations of his life. Many of the current accounts have become attempts to rehabilitate Jesus in the eyes of the larger secular or humanist society. Like many others, I follow this literature and am fascinated by what scholars can tell us about the life of Jesus. But we should stand back and ask ourselves, *What can we conclude from this scholarship? What is new that we have not seen in the scholarship of the past one hundred and fifty years?* And when we do so, we have to conclude that not much in this literature is new at all, despite the fact that many of these studies are presented as ground-breaking, or promoted as innovative challenges to so-called traditional belief.[11] These studies offer little that is new but, nevertheless, garner our acute attention. As an audience, we too are hoping for a rehabilitation of Jesus in the eyes of secular humanist society, but the approach these books are taking never seems to bring the issue any closer to being resolved.

Jesus, a Marginal Figure

MANY OF THE lives of Jesus since the latter part of the 20th century have presented Jesus as a marginal figure, peripheral to the Hebraic society of the day in which he was a minor revolutionary, a rebel leader, a minor sage, a wandering cynic influenced by

Hellenic thought, or marginal because he came from Galilee. From an historical point of view, however, this line of reasoning does not seem well-founded. For Jesus' movement to have had the relatively widespread impact it did before the fall of Jerusalem in 70 AD, as the writings of Paul attest, it is practically speaking not possible for Jesus to have been a marginal figure within the Palestine of the time. If it were possible to find a historian unfamiliar with Christian history and present to him/her all the primary sources and evidence on the growth of Christianity, and then to ask that historian to evaluate the likelihood that Jesus was a relatively insignificant figure in Palestine who made no widespread impact on his society while he was alive, the answer would be "Not very likely."

We must, then, ask ourselves why it is that there seems to be such a desire amongst writers who look at the Jesus question to portray him as a marginal figure in the recesses of the social and geo-political world of Palestine of the time. I think our first clue to answering this question comes when we look at the people who write these histories and ask what it is about the life of Jesus that they wish to ignore or downplay. The passion narrative is the single, dominant event in the life of Jesus reported in subsequent literature.[12] It forms the centre of his life in remembrances of him by those who wrote about him and in the traditions that were orally passed down and written within a few decades of his death in Jerusalem.

In all the various attempts to rehabilitate Jesus in the eyes of modern secular society, it is his ethical lessons and teaching, his sayings, and works as a healer, sage, or even country magician that are emphasized; it is not the passion of Jesus, his death and suffering narrative. Clearly, the passion narrative is a source of embarrassment, and the wish to rehabilitate Jesus in the eyes of secular/humanist society necessitates playing down the accounts of his death. What is left is an account of someone who was on the fringes of the Hebraic society of the time, someone working in the country, a minor figure.

Nino Ricci's Human Jesus

Literary critics have often cited as a mark of literary genius the ability of a writer to reflect currents within the society which epitomise its uniqueness. Nino Ricci offers such rare insight in his novel, *Testament,* a work that reflects current thinking on the historical Jesus in our society. We find here a remarkably vivid portrayal of a Jesus who is that marginal figure. We see him presented in his own situation in his own historical setting. What Ricci gives us is a human figure: a portrait that makes the reader intensely aware of Jesus' humanity.

A pre-eminent writer of contemporary fiction, Ricci's first book *Lives of the Saints* has become one of the most popular Canadian novels of all time and has been widely translated. Two subsequent novels, *In a Glass House* and *Where She Has Gone,* form a trilogy with *Lives of the Saints,* chronicling the life of an Italian immigrant boy, Vittorio.

In a postscript to *Testament,* Ricci acknowledges that he has been influenced by contemporary critical writing on Jesus, particularly the writings of the Jesus Seminar. Ricci's Jesus bears the mark of contemporary Jesus scholarship, particularly Jesus as a minor figure leading a marginal movement within the Palestine of the time. The book draws on details of some of this research and offers highly realistic descriptions of relationships with Roman and Hebrew authorities, the workings of the Temple priesthood in Jerusalem, and rural and village life.

Ricci's portrayal stands in contrast to what we might think

of as a Gospel portrayal or classical cinematic portrayal such as in Zefferelli's *Jesus of Nazareth* or Gibson's *The Passion of the Christ.* Ricci presents a man living with problems. He is like us; we do not have difficulty identifying with him. His problems are common problems and he feels them with the same intensity that we all feel. He is caught, as we are, trying to negotiate a way through all the various interests, resentments, desires, and ambitions of the people around him, their political motivations and what they expect and demand of him. And he is caught in the conflict between what he feels he is personally capable of and what he truly wants to achieve. This is not to say that this Jesus is not a man of empathy; he certainly is, to a degree that we might expect only to find in the rare person. Although the reader can identify and sympathize with Ricci's Jesus as a fellow human being, we see that he is not an average person from the strength of his own dedication to his principles and the lengths to which he is willing to go to follow his vision.

This character is a natural fit for Ricci. His Vittorio, particularly in the second and third novels of his trilogy, *In a Glass House* and *Where She Has Gone,* is a character in many respects like this Jesus: someone caught in his own predicament with a heightened sense of the entrapping contingency of human life; that is, the sense that every aspect of life is dependent upon the physical and social environment in which one operates. His character stands somewhat in contrast to that of the Jesus we know from the Gospel portrayals: where we find a person who, though faced with dramatic and extreme problems, is able to stand above conflict, above the trials and tribulations that amass to the point where most people would find them intolerable. The Jesus of the Gospels is remarkable in his ability to stand aside from the sense of the oppressiveness of human contingency; he is able to look upon his own environment from the perspective of what he sees as eternal goals and principles.

If we consider the Gospels and other New Testament writings separately from similar literature, we might regard the Jesus of the Gospels as somewhat unrealistic: a dramatized figure created only to promote the ideals of a movement. However, when we consider his life in comparison to those of such figures as Mohammed, Indian saints and ascetics, or even the saints of the Christian Church, we see that Jesus shares characteristics with them all. When we look at contemporary figures whom we consider religious leaders or founders, such as Mother Teresa, Bishop Romero of El Salvador, Ramana Maharshi of India, or politico-religious figures like Gandhi, Martin Luther King, and Nelson Mandela, we see that they too seem to have the ability to stand apart from the oppressiveness of human contingency. This appears to be a universal characteristic of religious figures who have transformed their societies, as well as of non-religious figures who have been able to instil a sense of mission and gather a large following.

Jesus' Inescapable Human Contingency

THIS CHARACTERISTIC is absent in the Jesus Ricci has created in *Testament*. As this becomes increasingly apparent to the reader, it creates a tension within the narrative. Even after readers are able to get beyond the traditional picture they have of Jesus and enter into the character Ricci has created (which is eminently possible, because of Ricci's ability to absorb his reader in the narrative), even then, an implausible tension rises between this hyper-real character absorbed in his problems and the religious following he inspires through his dedication to his vision. For example, the Judas character of the novel has difficulty understanding how Jesus can treat the lepers, and so does the reader. Not that it is implausible for someone to be that selfless, but the way Ricci's Jesus feels the pressures around him does not speak of someone who is able to stand aside from physical and mental suffering and take a spiritual stance of putting things in perspective in terms of eternal ideals.

This is Ricci's great service to us in our attempt to understand the Jesus of the Jesus Seminar and similar scholarship. He portrays a Jesus for whom it is so important to be human that, when faced with insurmountable challenges, his response confirms his humanity even where we would expect similar religious leaders to persevere.

In each of us there is an expectation that people do, in fact, rise above their own contingency; people do this on a daily basis in certain aspects of their lives. Figures in history who have been able to instil a sense of their own spiritual presence, and figures who have been known to inspire movements, are those people who are able to overcome what we consider normal human contingency. At one and the same time, we would like to get confirmation that those exceptional people have experienced the same struggles which have prevented us from rising to a higher plane. In this sense, Ricci has given us the Jesus that we want to see; someone like us, thoroughly human, caught in his own problems and subject to normal human contingency.

I would think that the writers of the Jesus Seminar, Funk in particular,[13] would find Ricci's Jesus an accurate portrayal of the character of the historical Jesus and would think that in seeing this Jesus we would understand something more of ourselves. For writers of the Jesus Seminar, such a portrayal of a person caught in his/her own contingency can correct the erroneous Christian conception of Jesus as someone with extra-ordinary or extra-human characteristics.

From a purely historical point of view, I think it is just not probable that Jesus was a figure caught up in the daily struggle and unable to see beyond it. He was most certainly a figure like others known for their spiritual presence, even some who are alive today, such as Mandela: people who were seemingly impervious to hardship and the struggles and issues of their own identity. In all likelihood, the character of Jesus was quite close to the one of the Gospels as presented by the traditional Churches when they speak of his human character as separate from his divine character; that of an exceptional religious and spiritual person, the kind who appear only occasionally and inspire remarkable followings.

The Solution Lives of Jesus

A PARALLEL GROUP of people who write on Jesus are those who write what I would call the solution narratives, or Solution Lives of Jesus. There is a spate of these works, many of which seem to be dramatically popular for a very short time, and all of which centre on or pick up on a particular part or fragment of Jesus lore or history or reference in biblical or later non-biblical writings. An isolated fragment is then presented as the answer to the question of who Jesus really was and why he had such an impact on the next two millennia. Barbara Thiering's account that Jesus was associated with the Qumran monastic movement is a prominent example. Thoroughly researched, it provides a useful comparison of ideas between the Qumran sect and early Christianity, but on the whole fails in its argument to reduce

34

Jesus to a product of this ascetic and mystical movement.[14]

With these solution lives of Jesus, there is a great temptation for scholars to think they have uncovered information that, once brought to the attention of the public, will lead to a new understanding of convictions long held within western culture. Many of these works are entertaining, and although some of their authors do for a short time enjoy some celebrity, their long-term impact is negligible. Part of their attraction is that there are a lot of questions to answer about the life of Jesus, particularly outside of the passion narrative.

The reason for the success of the solution lives, I think, lies in each of us, in the questioning that arises in us when we consider the challenges inherent in the Jesus story: especially the challenge of how a human being can represent for us personally, and as a society, a point of entry to the divine. When facing this challenge we naturally consider the option of discounting the passion narrative, from which it would follow that some other explanation must be found for the impact of Jesus on history. If we can find that explanation, then, of course, we can conclude that the passion is less relevant, and along with it, its far more challenging and far more provocative ensuing narratives of resurrection and appearance.

De-emphasis on the Passion Narrative

IN CONTEMPORARY CRITICAL writing on Jesus we find an explicit de-emphasising of the passion narratives as centrally portrayed in the four canonical Gospels. I think this comes about primarily because of the ideological stance of the anti-faith bias which regards the passion narrative as an embarrassment. Several explanations can be put forward for this de-emphasis. One is that it is not only the passion narratives but particularly the resurrection and appearance sequences which writers find embarrassing, and consequently the passion narratives themselves are questioned. If this story can be put in doubt, then there is no reason to offer any sort of empirical account of the resurrection and appearance sequences. Another explanation is the push to discount New Testament writings altogether and to look primarily to source literature and trace oral or written sources within these sources. By turning to source literatures, particularly of the synoptic Gospels, Gnostic and later literatures, these writings can be presented as truer, more accurate, and less doctored accounts of the life of Jesus; and, of course, as we have explained above, by taking this approach scholars can, in effect, write their own history of Jesus and of Christianity.

Paul and the Passion

ONE PROBLEM THAT remains to be resolved by taking the approach of other literatures outside of the canon, or source literatures, is the rather universal acceptance of the validity of the letters of Paul, which are regarded as the earliest Christian writings. The idea that the passion narrative was developed and in circulation when Paul was writing, either orally or in written form, is casually passed over by some writers, particularly certain ones associated with the Jesus Seminar. The assumption, or suggestion, is that the story of the passion, as we understand it from the four canonical Gospels, could not have taken place because it is not presented in Paul. This casual argument seems to have gathered widespread acceptance in critical circles.

Luke Timothy Johnson in his *The Real Jesus* has taken this

36

argument to task. He has shown that more or less the entire line of the passion narrative is assumed in the letters of Paul and other New Testament texts apart from the Gospels.[15] Traditionally, when the writings of Paul are read in a church setting, they are read against a backdrop of the story of the passion and death of Jesus. While some contemporary critics have dismissed this, Johnson has made a very good argument that this is in fact the case: that, as they were written, the letters of Paul assumed a knowledge of the passion story. I think critics have good reason to question this conclusion. The life of Jesus as presented in the synoptic Gospels from birth through death and resurrection and appearance has elements of fabrication, some of which are there to facilitate a completeness. In particular, the birth and childhood accounts cannot be corroborated through the writings of Paul. While critics have expounded the idea that the birth and childhood narratives, perhaps apart from some references to birthplace and parents' names, are additions, they have also extended this argument to the passion narrative. I believe Johnson has presented a convincing argument that the letters of Paul, written before 70 CE, presuppose and thus corroborate the passion narrative.

Johnson and Wright on Contemporary Critical Writing on Jesus

I FIND CONVINCING Johnson's assessment of critical writings on the life of Jesus and the way he addresses the issue of what we can really know. Similarly, the work of N.T. Wright also appears to me to be well balanced in its evaluation of these same writings. Their view is that the death narratives as we know them in most of their detail are accurate. Both

Johnson and Wright survey the major works by scholars associated with the Jesus Seminar and other prominent New Testament scholars, and they examine the important early literatures, the Dead Sea Scrolls, and the Nag Hammadi texts, and review what these can tell us about Jesus and his times. Johnson also looks at other literature dating from the time of the early Church and afterward, and gives an account of the earlier extra-Christian sources.[16]

The huge body of literature on the historical Jesus stretching back more than one hundred and fifty years has led to many questions and few answers. Whenever an account of the life of Jesus as a human being living in Palestine is presented to us, it always carries a certain controversy, no matter how many times these accounts are re-presented. It seems clear to me, as I think it did to Schweitzer, and does to Johnson and Wright, that the answer to what stimulates the controversy lies more in the people who are reading and writing the lives of Jesus of Nazareth than in the historical accuracy of these lives.

Jesus and the Sacramental

LIKE PEOPLE IN the mid-19th century, we live knowing that Jesus was a human being and at the same time that he represents for us an entry into the divine. People in Renan's Paris of 1863 were searching, as we are, to resolve two irreconcilable needs within ourselves. We see in every human being the desire for some type of reconciliation between our own religious and spiritual requirements and our own deterministic, empiricist make-up that interprets for us the seemingly physically finite reality in which we live. Jesus in the personage of Jesus of Nazareth, as he came to be known to us through early

Christian writings, has become for us that person, that symbol in western culture, the point at which we overcome the irreconcilable aspects of our personal religious and deterministic character.

The sacramental is one of several arguments put forward by the Church over the centuries to explain this reconciliation. There is nothing new or revolutionary here; it is a basic Christian concept and one shared with every major religious faith and religious manifestation. We know it particularly in Christianity through the sacrament, the point at which there is some entry into the beyond; in the language of the Church, the symbol of an "outward grace," where the divine can touch a sense of humanity. We look particularly for the sacramental in certain physical things, we focus on particular physical objects, and we say here is the entry into another level of existence. We find this in India in the simple acts of *puja* where people offer a bit of rice before an image of the deity; in the incense of a makeshift shrine before the Buddha at the back of a shop; in the circumambulation of the Ka'ba in Mecca by hundreds of thousands; we see it in Christianity in the Eucharist, a traditional meal that celebrates the passion of Jesus. These two sides of our nature as humans, the religio-spiritual and deterministic, will never be fully reconciled. People are religious and spiritual beings, and people are deterministic and empiricist beings who are more than aware of their own contingency and more than determined not to let themselves be limited by it.

39

1   See Edgar Hennecke, ed., *New Testament Apocrypha,* rev. edition, ed. Wilhelm Schneemelcher; English translation, ed. R. McL. Wilson (Louisville, Ky.: Westminster/John Knox Press, 1991-92, 2 v.).

2   For a brief summary of these literatures see Luke Timothy Johnson, *The Real Jesus* (New York: HarperSanFrancisco, 1997), p. 88-9, 147-51.

3   John Dominic Crossan, *The Historical Jesus: The Life of a Mediterranean Jewish Peasant* (New York: HarperCollins, 1992).

4   John P. Meier, *A Marginal Jew: Rethinking the Historical Jesus* (N.Y.: Doubleday, 1991, 1994, 2 v.); Burton Mack, *The Lost Gospel: The Book of Q and Christian Origins* (San Francisco: HarperSanFrancisco, 1993).

5   Ernest Renan, *Vie de Jésus* (Paris: Calmann-Lévy, 1964).

6   Henri Barbusse, *Jésus* (Paris: Flammarion, 1927).

7   A sampling of such approaches is provided by William E. Arnal and Michel Desjardins, eds., *Whose Historical Jesus?* (Waterloo: Wilfrid Laurier University Press, 1997).

8   Albert Schweitzer, *The Quest for the Historical Jesus,* ed. John Bowden (Minneapolis: Fortress Press, 2001).

9   Marcus J. Borg and N.T. Wright, *The Meaning of Jesus: two visions* (San Francisco: HarperSanFrancisco, 1999). Also of note in this connection is a similar work, John Dominic Crossan, Luke Timothy Johnson and Werner H. Kelber, *The Jesus Controversy* (Harrisburg, PA: Trinity Press, 1999).

10 The view that religious expression is a primitive response to the universe and that progress in society leads to an increasingly scientific and rational interpretation of the world.

11 For example, A. N. Wilson, *Jesus* (London: Sinclair-Stevenson, 1992); or, John Shelby Spong, *Resurrection: myth or reality? a bishop's search for the origins of Christianity* (San Francisco: HarperSanFrancisco, 1994).

12 Johnson, p. 133-40.

13 *The Five Gospels: the search for the authentic words of Jesus,* eds. Robert W. Funk, Roy W. Hoover, and the Jesus Seminar (New York: HarperSanFrancisco, 1993).

14 Barbara Thiering, *Jesus and the Riddle of the Dead Sea Scrolls* (Toronto: Doubleday, 1992). Similarly, see J.M. Allegro, *The Sacred Mushroom and the Cross: A Study of the Nature and Origins of Christianity within the Fertility Cults of the Near East* (London: Hodder and Stoughton, 1970).

15 Johnson, p. 117-22. Donald Akenson makes the case for Paul's familiarity with the ministry of Jesus, as well as the passion. See his *Saint Saul: a skeleton key to the historical Jesus* (New York: Oxford/Kingston: McGill-Queens, 2000), p, 171-211.

16 I could certainly guide the reader to examine two short books, Johnson's *The Real Jesus* and N.T. Wright's, *Who Was Jesus* (Grand Rapids, Mich.: Eerdmans, 1993). Two of what I consider to be sober and appropriately critical accounts of Christian sources, these books take us as far as we can reasonably go in terms of what can be known about the historical Jesus and also take that extra step of critically examining why writers, like those associated with the Jesus Seminar, have gone in directions they have.

2

CRITICAL BELIEVERS

T HERE IS A general theory of the decline of religion
that floats about in popular culture. It is called secularization. The theory goes something like this:

Religion has been steadily on the decline since the rise
of rational and scientific thought, a process that started
amongst intellectuals, thinkers and philosophers at the
time of the Italian Renaissance, and began to take hold
more widely during the Age of Enlightenment in the
18th century with the beginning of scientific thinking
and a truer understanding of the planetary systems
through the advances in astronomy and physics brought
about by Galileo's theories and Newton's discovery of
the law of gravity. The process was given a significant
boost on the political level by the French revolution,
but really took hold when people began to understand
their universe in the 19th century with the rise of biological studies, and associated scientific discoveries cul-
minating in the evolutionary theories of Darwin. Late
in the 19th century, secularization was well on its way as
a transformative societal process as evidenced by the
work of sociological thinkers like Durkheim, but people
as a whole really didn't understand the secular nature of

the universe and gain a true appreciation for the word until the mid-20th century, when the fruits of scientific thinking finally reached the masses. After World War II, participation in religion declined, and the blind faith, which had heretofore been the cloak of ignorance over all of mankind, was finally reduced to influencing only the naive in our society, but, unfortunately, still held sway over the developing world, where compulsory public education has yet to be introduced.

Many courses on secularization have been taught in universities, where it has developed into a sub-discipline of its own. I took one of these courses myself in graduate school. Fortunately, my professor, Thomas McIntire, presented this material for what it was: allowing his students to see the inconsistencies and the positivist tendencies within the theory.

Religious Participation

ACCORDING TO secularization theory, there ought to be a notable decline over the years in the rate of participation in religious services and rites of all faiths and a corresponding decline in the rate of belief in a deity. Advocates of secularisation theory draw much of their support from participation rates in the western world from the post-WWII period to the present day. Here a clear trend can be found in declining participation in all major Christian churches in North America and elsewhere. Participation rates are, of course, collected according to varying definitions and differ by age group, denomination and region and tend to be based on participation in a religious service or function in the recent

past (typically over a number of weeks). In general, such surveys show a decline from mid-century highs in the United
States of approximately 50%, down to 30%, while Canada has
lower corresponding numbers, with declines from approximately 40% to 20%. In Europe, where participation figures
have traditionally been lower than in North America, they
have fallen from the teens down to single digits.

Statistics on participation have been collected by well-known
commentators on religion; in the United States by Andrew
Greeley,[1] in Canada by Reginald Bibby, and in Britain by
Callum G. Brown. In Canada, Bibby has regularly published the
results of his surveys over the past couple of decades, carefully
demonstrating declines in participation, and has forcefully made
the argument of an encroaching secularization, until his 2002
book, in which he presents evidence for a reversal of this trend
in Canada.[2] The face of religion in Canada has been changing
on account of changing demographics: most visibly through
immigration and the introduction of significant numbers of
people practising world religions other than Christianity and
Judaism. But Bibby points to several other factors as well, such as
youth participation and a return to religion in sectors where it
would not have been expected. He therefore comes to the conclusion that, strictly speaking, there is no pattern of declining
religious participation in Canada.[3] From this he draws the larger
conclusion that religion is not on a path toward extinction.

Despite evidence such as that presented by Bibby, advocates
of secularization hold to their theory, rightly pointing out
that figures still show massive declines in participation since
WWII. But participation rates prior to WWII, where they do
exist, present another set of problems for the theory.
Although somewhat spotty, the best figures available for any
one country pertain to Britain, where participation rates can

be surmised from a number of different surveys and sources going back to the beginning of the 19th century. When we look at these figures, we can see that participation has risen and fallen a number of times, depending principally upon societal responses to crises, such as war, and changes in religious practice, such as the rise of Methodism and Evangelicalism.

The most stunning evidence presented by these figures is that, contrary to the picture proponents of secularization are fond of painting, which typically extends back only to the post-WWII era, rates of participation were, in fact, never "high" and barely, if ever, represented a majority of the population in Britain. Figures for the past two hundred years have hovered in the 20% to 30% range, although they are somewhat lower currently. Those survey numbers and other historical records that are available, such as birth, baptismal, marriage and death registries, from which figures can be gleaned for the past two centuries for various European countries, present no evidence that there ever was a sustained majority of the population participating in religion.[4]

Religion and Doing History

HOW WE THINK about history has played a role in accentuating the dominance of religious worldviews and the view of the predominance of faith in past ages. While this is a perennial problem, it has served to abnormally heighten the the impression of a decline of the religious worldview in the 20th century.

History naturally seeks to look at major "shaping" events — crises, catastrophic occurrences — which aid the historian in characterising a time or a people. History cannot be reproduced in all its detail, and consequently, dominant issues and

leaders come to the fore in historical portraiture, and exceptions
to the rule tend to be left by the wayside. When issues related
to religion are looked at by historians, what we get are leaders'
positions: official statements on God by the state or a king
exhibiting the influence of religious figures such as the Pope or
Reformation leaders. History also tends to move from one crisis
to another, from war to famine and so on: events which tend to
solicit religiously flavoured statements on the part of leaders
because the public, religious and non-religious alike, have an
appetite for them in times of crisis. If we were to use these types
of crises as the markers of contemporary society — media reports
on terrorist attacks, statements by the President of the United
States, such as the State of Union Address or a declaration of
war, reports of famine in Africa, news reports of massacres, and
so on — we would find that prominent in all of these is the
position of religious leaders, appeals to God or for prayer, or
expressions of outrage from the Churches in response to war or
other calamities.

We tend to take these statements as a matter of course. In
most cases, we do not retain any personal memory of them.
Nevertheless, a browse through media reports shows they are
very frequently present. If asked what the influence of religious leaders and religious attitudes of society was, surrounding such events, I think the average person would assign a relatively low level of significance to these statements. But from
the vantage point of a hundred or two hundred years, when
we look into the past where historical reports are the only
reconstructive tools available, then statements of religious
leaders and religious attitudes of society take on a higher
prominence. From an historical point of view, if such records
are all that exists, it may be nearly impossible to discern an
accurate picture of religious attitudes of the time. But in

periods where abundant historical records are available, it is clear that the influence of religion on societal attitudes was, in most cases, far less predominant than would be suggested by a survey of historical records relating to seminal events. For example, a summary of the statements of Henry VIII on his religious reforms, as opposed to a recent scholarly biography, would leave a reader with very different, and often contradictory, conclusions on the influence of religion on societal attitudes in Tudor England.

Belief in Spiritual Reality

ANOTHER ASPECT OF secularization theory posits the decline in belief in a deity, Supreme Being, or spiritual reality. Here again secularization theorists[5] have difficulty supporting their arguments from statistical surveys. Rates of belief have stayed consistently in the 70% to 80% range, not only since the time of WWII, but going back to the 19th century.[6]

The other problematic aspect for secularization theory is the turnover rate. Many churches report relatively high turnover rates in their participating membership. People also tend to participate in religion at different times in their lives, sometimes surrounding the religious education of their children, sometimes at periods associated with rites of passage such as marriage, baptism, or at times of the loss of a loved one, and in old age. If a survey were to ask: *Have you ever participated in a religious service and do you believe in a spiritual reality?* there would be a positive response from a majority of all populations in Canada, in the United States and in Europe. But it is unlikely that at any time in history there would ever have been a majority responding positively to questions about a personal relationship to a personal deity, such as: *Do you believe in Jesus Christ as a divine person who was sent by God to save the world and that through Him you will gain your salvation?*

It is the false assumption, that in the not too distant past a majority of the population would have answered yes to this question, which feeds the secularization theory.

Although it is generally assumed in modern western society that religion is on the decline, I do think this assumption in our day is not owing to the arguments of theorists of any kind, but is part of our development as people and, in particular, our development from childhood to adulthood. Inherent in our development into adults is the projection of a veil of religious belief which we attribute to our parents and forebears and even to history itself. It plays a large part in societal views on religion, and may, I think, be strong enough to cloud what we know through experience and from history.

Where does this leave us? It leads to conclusions that fly in the face of secularization theory: first, that at any given time only a minority of people have ever participated in religion; and second, that at any time in the past, as currently, religion has had a profound effect on most people at some point in their lives.

Religion and Spirituality

AS WE HAVE seen, there is a major difference in the approach people take toward participation in religion and toward a belief in a spiritual reality. If we want to look at society as a whole and characterize it, we would have to say that only a minority of people participate in religion, while a majority hold to a belief in a spiritual reality. *Can people be both religious (or non-religious) and spiritual to seemingly contradictory ends?* and if so, *What, then, is religion?* and *What is spirituality?* and *How do they differ?*

Opinions have diverged somewhat among scholars on the question *What is religion?* Scholars who have tried to define religion have arrived at a handful of elements which they posit as having to be present in order to label an activity a religion or a religious practice. These might include: ritual, community, belief in a deity (theism), principles of ethical behaviour, a priesthood, or holy sites. It might be argued that any one of these elements is not a requirement for a religion. Yet, the three that I would suggest are necessary are ritual, community and deity.

Likewise, spirituality has been examined in several different ways by scholars. For our purposes, when we speak generally of the spirituality of a person, spirituality can be understood in the simplest terms as a desire for a relationship with the transcendent.

While I do think these definitions are accurate, on a personal level, I don't think they are helpful. When we come to ask ourselves the questions *Am I a religious person? Am I a spiritual person? Am I religious person who participates in religion? Am I person with a spiritual dimension?* then definitions like those above are left behind.

In my understanding, to be a religious person includes two elements which can be attributed to people who participate in religion throughout the world and in all the major religious faiths. The first would be that people hold to the principle of non-harm, according to which their activities, active or passive, should never cause harm, or deprivation of good, to others. This principle would imply that personal gain or profit could never be taken at the expense of another even if this were considered the greater good. The second requisite element for a religious person is the understanding that there is an aspect of creation which is fallen. An understanding of the world as

49

existing in some measure apart from its true or proper nature is central to every major religious faith.

To be a spiritual person, and again I would say this holds true for all major religious faiths, is to be a person who has a continuing desire for a sacramental relationship to the transcendent reality in which the world is perfected.

The Human Condition

PART AND PARCEL of life as a spiritual being is the recognition of an inherent non-fit between what we recognize as the reality of our daily life and the world of possibility with which our lives as spiritual beings seek to engage. Philosophers have always puzzled over this quandary. Plato is perhaps the best known in this regard for his postulating of a world of realities of which the material world is only a phantom. We find it powerfully represented in the 20th century writer Albert Camus, where it forms the central theme of most of his novels. This quandary is perhaps better known as the human condition. Many writers have offered their own particular take on this, but to provide a broad explanation that would cover the main issues in philosophical and religious thought for our purposes, it might be understood as the situation where we find ourselves perpetually caught between human contingency or compromise and what we can see as a metaphysical possibility.

When we reflect philosophically, most of us can readily identify with this quandary, because we are confronted with a difficult world in which we find no clear path to justice. We nurture convictions of belief in a world of hope and possibility; and we find such a world necessary in order to cope with the "counter-world" of competing interests, competing "goods," in which we live.

Knowing this to be our experience, and faced with the answers that religion and in particular that the Christian Church has provided for us in the form of Jesus Christ and the theological explanations which have developed out of the Church's understanding of Jesus' biblical experience, we cannot help but respond critically to theological tenets and principles as presented, and, in particular, respond critically to the life of Jesus and its accompanying Creed. Taken blindly, these principles and tenets offer a complete response to the problems we apprehend as the human condition. Seen through the lens of the human condition, our age is not so much one of a "loss of faith" as much as it is an age in which it has become not only legitimate and acceptable, but even necessary, to critically examine our faith.

In Canadian, American and European society, a social secularism holds sway in popular discourse. Social secularism is the politically correct. It is socially acceptable, but I would have to say that it is not the norm. As I have shown, a majority in modern western society confess to a spiritual dimension in their lives. We are spiritual beings who readily admit to either the existence of a personal deity or a belief in a transcendent reality. We populate an age of critical believers. We are not a society that accepts without question the tenets of the Christian Churches, or of other religions; and at the same time, we are not secularists accepting as sufficient a deterministic explanation for a world which limits us to a mundane existence.

We are critical believers. This is how we respond to the problems and confusions of daily life; this is how we respond to the problem of the human condition; this is how we respond to Jesus Christ as the answer, the answer provided by the Churches.

Loss-of-Faith Spectrum

IF CRITICAL BELIEF adequately describes the situation in which most of us find ourselves, this begs the question: *What has shifted in the faith versus non-faith landscape?*

At one extreme is the notion of blind faith: a notion which accepts that the Churches are the custodians of a Truth given to them as revelation from God, held in sacred texts, and explained through Church teachings. On taking this position, faith becomes simple, yet this works for relatively few in our society. Faith is often understood in these simple terms, as a take-it-or-leave-it option. As such, it is presented as something you have or you don't. This faith versus non-faith dichotomy has lived a long life despite the fact that most cannot operate within its bounds. Its proponents make for very strange bedfellows.

Virtually all the Christian Churches from the evangelical through the mainline Churches, Christian writers and theologians throughout history, along with today's most adamant anti-theists and secularists (including communists), support the same model of the faith versus non-faith dichotomy. Despite what appears to be a preponderance of opinion, surveys on belief in a transcendent reality show that the faith most people have does not fit, for the most part, the mould of this dichotomy.[7] Moreover, a critical look at history shows that people always were far more sophisticated in their views on the complexities of faith. It is strange to see secularists like Freud and a host of anti-theist biblical scholars alongside leaders of the traditional Christian Churches all holding to the same dichotomy and pronouncing that if you do not unquestioningly believe in the biblical Christ as found in Church doctrines then you have lost your faith.

Gaining and protecting a healthy faith has become imbued in Christian discourse. The archetypal warning beacon for it in Christianity is the Apostle Thomas, known as Doubting Thomas, who is somehow considered to be less than Christian because he carried his doubts with him. The notion of faith as a complete or blind faith is very often tied to a belief in the veracity of the biblical accounts which must be accepted in their totality, including miraculous events and/or explanations and stories which we know to be contrary to the laws of nature.

As a student at McGill, I took a course with Professor Bob Culley on the Hebrew Scriptures. Some of the students in this class were candidates for ordination in evangelical denominations. An uncomfortable silence descended over the first few classes as Professor Culley began to dissect a biblical text, showing specific passages to be interpolations and suggesting that in consequence of faulty manuscript copying, and even faulty grammar, different words had been inserted. He began to meet with a certain amount of resistance on the part of some of the students, who claimed that their approach to the Bible was to accept it in its totality and that this represented for them a Truth. If they could not take it as a totality, then the Bible would lose all semblance of truth.

Professor Culley, no doubt having faced this situation before, pointed out the inconsistency of the argument. If scripture was going to represent a Truth, or the foundation of faith, it did not follow that faith and/or truth was destroyed if one could show problems with part of the text. The point Professor Culley was making for the students was that as biblical scholars their responsibility was to take biblical literature for what it was, to examine it within its own context and to see what it had to offer; and, similarly, the scholar had to guard against imposing interpretations on the text.

Despite certain overtures within theological circles to critical reflection on faith, such as the theological concept of healthy doubt, the faith versus non-faith dichotomy has persisted. One can often hear theological writers, or even anti-theists and secularists, speaking of a progression in loss of faith. One may hear descriptions of a movement from doubt to anger to incomprehension, which advocates of the Church might describe as the dangers of loss of faith, while secularists would describe it as a progression to enlightenment or a casting off of religious ignorance — for both groups, it is a movement between two extremes. At one end is faith, in which belief is described as something passed down, accepted, and centred on God and God's role in the universe. It may come to people through a conversion experience, a response to a personal crisis of loss, or existential angst, or it may be a confirmation of the immanence of the transcendent in this world.[8] At the other extreme is non-faith, in which one has thrown off the cloak of religious ignorance and come to the understanding that there is no transcendent reality which has a governing role or plan for the world and its individuals.

The first stage in the loss-of-faith progression between these two extremes is doubt; doubt that questions God's love and individualized care for people. For the theist, this is a state of caution in which one can come back from the brink through diligent prayer. For secularists, these are the first moments of enlightenment when one questions ignorance. The second stage is that of anger, when one responds to God on a personal level and a breach of the relationship with the deity may occur. The final stage before complete loss of faith is that of identifying widespread injustice as evidence of the lack of transcendent guidance in the universe. This would be where one is struck by the inevitability of social strife and realizes that true justice is simply not possible in the world in which we live, and one then draws the conclusion that God cannot exist because God must be the embodiment of justice.

I was once shocked to hear a priest I knew say that the thing he feared and hated most was to have someone come to confession and say they had lost their faith. His reason was that there was nothing he could do for a person in this position. Consequently, it left him feeling useless and unable to carry out his role as a priest. At the time I was shocked because I found it a senseless position to take on his part. What was his role, I thought, if not to talk to people about their faith? His response also seemed completely inexplicable to me because I knew him to be a person with a completely practical view of life, a person far from doctrinaire, open and accommodating to people of all faiths and a friend to everyone regardless of their attitude toward religion. Recalling this after the benefit of years, and under-standing him to be the person he was, I see that his point was more likely that he felt unable to help people who were trapped in the faith versus non-faith dichotomy. When he encountered such a person he may have found that the dichotomy was so ingrained that it was virtually impossible to pry them out of the mind-set.

The Scientific Worldview

APART FROM THE work of proponents of secularisation theory, there is also an understanding prevalent in society that advance-ments in the sciences and particularly in the natural sciences have quietly superseded any sort of religious explanation about the world and the universe and why we are here.[9]

If we were to ask what had the most significant effect on the popularity of the religious worldview during the 20th century, I think we would have to conclude that it was not the rise of the scientific worldview or even the World Wars, but rather, two very practical transformations in our societies. The first is that we have swung from being a predominantly rural and agrarian society to being a predominantly urban one. At the beginning of the 20th century, 60% to 70% of the population in the western world lived in rural areas and only a very few received any post-secondary education. By the end of the 20th century, the structure of rural-urban society had completely switched to where 70% to 80% were urban dwellers and, for the first time, a majority of the population was gaining post-secondary education. The other radical transformation in modern society, which occurred at roughly the same time, was the decline of religious institutions' involvement in the delivery of social services and education. Prior to 1900, the majority of schools, hospitals, and what we think of as the welfare state, along with relief from catastrophic occurrences (natural disasters, fire, etc.), were largely administered by religious organizations. Their role, though still significant in 1950, had all but disappeared a generation later. Rural society was heavily dependent upon church organisations to maintain social infrastructure in social services, health, and education. Changes in these social structures have directly led to the decline of the moral influence the Churches have had over society and to the corresponding disregard for the worldview they represent.

While many would assume that the battle for predominance between the religious and the scientific worldviews is new, and is a particular hallmark of the 20th century, in fact, this conflict is perennial. It can be found in literature going back centuries. It was prevalent among the ancient Greeks, and we even find it in the Christian scriptures.

The most obvious case is that of the confrontation recounted in *The Acts of the Apostles* of Paul and Epicureans and Stoics in

Athens. The conflict is played out much more openly in Gospel narratives, particularly those of the miracles. What is the account of the "loaves and fishes" if not an explicit statement of the contradiction between a belief in a deity who intercedes in the empirical realm on behalf of adherents, and the known patterns of behaviour of the physical world?

The life of Galileo is perhaps the most celebrated example in history of the conflict of the scientific worldview with the religious. Galileo's conflict with the Church is often referred to in terms of two clearly opposing positions.[10] Galileo's arguments, however, were sophisticated and his presentation of them calculated and subtle. Apart from any intellectual argument he was proposing, also at play was his desire to do battle with the Church to win over public opinion. Nevertheless, Galileo did want to move beyond the issues of simple conflict over the biblical explanation of the universe; he wanted to move to a position of having the Church, and the public, understand that their claims to religious and spiritual realities were not dependent upon physical and scientific realities. This being the case, his claim to have agreed with the Church on the basic tenets of the Christian faith may well have been genuine.

Many examples of the conflict between religious and scientific worldviews can be found in the writings of the Church Fathers from the mid-second century through the third century. St. Augustine's *Doctrina Christiana*, for example, carefully argues the shortcomings of history and the natural sciences. From even earlier, perhaps the best example comes from the ancient Roman world in the writings of Lucretius, particularly in his *De Rerum Natura*, a brilliant epic piece in which the ignorance and idiocies of the religious outlook are shown for what they are in Lucretius' estimation as compared to rational and logical thought.

57

Darwin — Marx — Freud

IN OUR TIME, three major intellectual movements have been championed as developments that might show how a deterministic -empiricist worldview could usurp a religious understanding of the world. These are evolution, best exemplified by Charles Darwin; socialism, most forcefully presented as communism by Karl Marx; and psychology, best known and presented in its extreme view by Sigmund Freud.

The theory of the evolution of life through natural selection is now largely identified with the efforts of Darwin in the 19th century. His now-famous reports on the life-forms isolated through the centuries on the Galapagos Islands fascinated the public and allowed people to comprehend in a single theory much of the work of the categorisation of the biological and zoological world that had developed through the efforts of amateurs in the 19th century. Although Darwin certainly had some public conflicts with religious leaders, the idea that his theories might be held up as a scientific worldview in opposition to a religious one was mainly left to Herbert Spencer, another popular thinker of the time. Although familiar only to historians today, Spencer was singularly responsible for the promotion of Darwin's ideas on natural selection. His views were aptly known, not as Darwinism, nor evolutionism, but as Spencerism. It was not until well into the 20th century, through various re-evaluations of Darwin's writings, and particularly his letters, that thinkers came to realize that presenting a scientific worldview in opposition to a religious understanding was in fact a motivator for Darwin himself in the promotion of his theories.

There have been many attempts at reconciling an evolutionary explanation for mankind with the accounts of creation found in the Hebrew scriptures. Perhaps the best-known is the work

Pierre Teilhard de Chardin (1881-1955), who, in *The Phenomenon of Man*, looked at the theory of evolution and discoveries in the natural sciences, particularly anthropology, as a reflection of a grander cosmological process which a divine setting-in-motion, and plan, had initiated.

Despite the great promise of evolutionary theory, of offering us an explanation of our origins, more comprehensive and detailed research in the latter part of the 20th century has uncovered many contradictions within its various iterations. While some theorists do acknowledge such contradictions, society has quietly come to accept as incontrovertible the notion that not only species, but all life, has evolved on earth. Just as significant has been the popular realization that some species may have de-evolved; sharks and alligators have remained frozen at certain stages while other life forms have continued to change. Strangely enough, the collective realization that life evolves has not allowed evolutionism to become the dominant and formative theory for people in the 20th century; rather, the seeming contradictions within evolutionary theories have left people with the empty conclusion that, although we are participants in evolution, we are not on a path of evolving into higher life forms.

The concept of socialism and the socialist experiments of the sharing of property and work have been around since ancient times, but as a political movement they never gained real strength until popular opposition arose in the 19th century to working conditions in Europe's emerging industrial centres. Marx, with his doctrinaire iteration of socialism as communism, has been the most influential spokesperson in this sphere and considered the greatest threat to a religious worldview. He characterized religion as a movement which, through the promotion of ignorance and pacification, co-opts people and enhances their susceptibility to manipulation by those in power. This understanding of religion he quaintly encapsulated in the phrase "opiate of the people." Because of long-standing socialist traditions in Christianity and other religions, many religious thinkers were quick to respond to Marx's attack on religion by pointing out the many successful examples of socialist living within religious traditions, such as monastic communities, which arose in opposition to secular and economic trends of urban centres in the middle ages, and Anabaptists (Mennonites), who withdrew from the society of the time to create self-sustaining communities in opposition to state control. Despite much hostility between the parties, there were those who thought that an accommodation with Marx's doctrine was possible. One of the best known of such thinkers was Dorothy Day, who through her writing and action laid the groundwork for a theoretical reconciliation of Christian charity and Communist distribution of goods.

Today the idea that a communist understanding of the world and mankind could be a threat to a religious worldview is hardly given any credence. A movement that only a generation ago many feared would overtake the world has experienced a drastic setback to its once near-universal influence. What has reduced Marxism's theoretical threat to a religious understanding of the world has not been its decline in political influence; rather, it has been the subsequent conclusions drawn about the economic self-interest of people. Part of the great experiment of communist countries was to flatten the social strata of the population and offer a relatively equivalent salary to members of the labour force. In the West, we have understood this to be the Achilles heel of the communist experiment, because we accept that economic motivation is essential not only to the material well-being of people and economies, but even to social well-being.

Major movements of protest against capitalism and economic hegemony, commonly regarded today in its vilest guise as global-ization, no longer advocate a radical transformation or revolu-tion; instead, their initiatives are in the much more modest forms of demands for regulation, transparency, and account-ability. This has left social reformers and protesters with the deflated conclusion that real redistribution of wealth can only come about through social transformations, i.e., secular humanism; but we have yet to see a coherent and convincing presentation of a secular theory of human transformation.

The last of the three most influential movements to present an alternative interpretation to the religious worldview in recent times is psychology. Just why psychology would have taken root so strongly in the late 19th century is somewhat curious, as there is very little in the theory that had not been put forth in previous centuries. Apart, perhaps, from a certain new materialistic understanding of the human being, which proposed that by studying the brain, we can understand the soul or spirit, or, in the new terminology, the psyche or ego of the human being. Of the many proponents of the new psychological interpretation, the best known was Freud. His theories became exemplary, per-haps because he was ready to draw conclusions where others hesi-tated in the face of the complexities and subtleties of the person. Consequently, his ideas were widely influential and taken up by practicing psychiatrists and psychologists. Much is made of Freud's division of the psyche into its constituent parts of id, ego and superego and his assertion that the key to understanding our relationships, particularly to our mothers and fathers, lies in deeply-hidden sexual motivations and desires: especially, in the primal desire for dominance relating back to an actual killing of the first father. Freud's psychology has brought about a more mechanistic understanding of a side of human nature that defies mechanism. Success for Freud and his followers has been in an alternative interpretation of the person to traditional religious ones. Whereas religious interpretations of the person have directed people to look outside themselves for answers to questions of origins, issues of meaning, judgement, and morality, psychology has told every person that they have the power to answer all these questions from within themselves.

As with Marxism, the controversy that arose between psychology and a religious interpretation of the world was immediate and played a large part in the professional and theoretical motivations of Freud and other early psychologists. Perhaps because much of the ground onto which Freudian psychology was treading was traditionally religious, and because much of psychology's language was religious, there were many attempts at reconciliation between the psychological and religious understandings of the person. The best known was that of Carl Jung (1875-1961), who looked to religious traditions, particularly of Asia, and to the large knowledge base and vocabulary of the emerging field of world religions and mythology, to identify archetypes. He used these archetypes, primal forms which have become universalized in all cultures, to encourage people to understand themselves by pursuing an inner spiritual quest. While psychology became increasingly influential in the latter part of the 20th century, the desire in popular culture for a purely psychological understanding of the person has quietly died away.

The Universality of Belief

AS A STUDENT at McGill I became acquainted with a priest through the Catholic Student Centre who had attracted something of a following because of his deep spirituality. He appeared to find it embarrassing when students began coming to the Centre specifically to hear him say mass. He was a Catholic Indian raised in a Hindu milieu and, as an academic, was an expert in Islam. He was a complex personality in other ways. Conversant on a broad range of issues both secular and religious, he was socially and in conversation a seemingly sophisticated man, despite the cloak of spirituality which hung about him and the openness of his deep personal devotion to Christ.

When he offered a series of seminars on his approach to world faiths, I was anxious to attend. I quickly became perplexed to hear him describe the religious practices of other faiths in a language I had expected him to reserve for his own Christian tradition. I don't believe I would have been so taken aback had he been a priest like some others, who approach the beliefs of other faiths in the dry and detached manner of the social sciences. I recall considering for some time whether I would ask him if he thought these faiths were "true," or if they were "valid." I cannot remember which I asked, and perhaps it does not matter, because he replied in a simple assertive way that they were. Having no reason to doubt him, I found it, in a way, revolutionary, because I had assumed that a move toward religious pluralism was a move toward a critical and limited rationalist view of religion.

I have since had the opportunity to meet other people, mostly from the East, whose personal deep religious convictions have allowed them to understand more fully the personal beliefs of people of other faiths, precisely because they have an appreciation for personal belief. This is an understanding difficult for someone from the West to acquire, and one of the valuable characteristics the religions of India have to offer.

The knowledge that an individual devotion, such as that of this priest for Christ, can live in harmony with a genuine pluralist view that respects multiple faiths brings home the point that people live among multiple religious cultures. But at the same time, the compatibility of an individual devotion with pluralism can also make one very much aware of the fundamental unity of religious belief.

This sense of unity or the oneness of belief, I think, also lies at the heart of the problem that I addressed in my first chapter. Our fascination with the historical Jesus is an expression in western culture of the sacramental relationship with the transcendent; and, I would emphasize, it is a religious expression indigenous to western culture. The fact of the historical Jesus is our identification of the point at which we meet the divine and our acknowledgement of the fundamental non-fit of a human and mortal reality with the truth and goodness that we believe exists elsewhere and ought to be within our grasp because it is within our understanding. We feel that our life, our world, has somehow fallen away from that truth and goodness, and that the oneness offered by the realization of the sacramental relationship with Jesus Christ may in some way repair that fallen aspect of our world. And so, as in other religions, we engage in rituals which celebrate a sacramental relationship to the divine. Despite the reality of our finiteness, we still seek that unity with the transcendent.

I do not suggest there is a simple religious solution to the dichotomy of a transcendent reality and the human world. As I have argued, people are critical believers. As critical believers we must take account of realities surrounding our understanding of faith: that there has always been a projection of near universal faith onto previous eras when there is no evidence to suggest this is true; that the current state of critical belief has been more or less the universal experience throughout history; that statistics on religious participation show that to have a minority participating

64

in organized religion is the norm; and that statistics also show that the majority of people hold to a belief in a transcendent reality, whether that be a personal belief or one in keeping with the theology of an organized religion.

Taking all this into account, we see that people can function with two aspects of their nature: a critical nature that takes full account of contingent reality; and a nature that recognizes belief in a possibility for goodness which exists in a fundamental non-fit, or non-compatibility, with the world of human relations.

---

1 Andrew Greeley, *Unsecular Man* (New York: Schocken, 1972).

2 Reginald W. Bibby, *Restless Gods: the renaissance of religion in Canada* (Toronto: Stoddard, 2002).

3 Peter Berger has also recently revised his views on the progress of secularization in western society. See his *Questions of Faith: a skeptical affirmation of Christianity* (Oxford: Blackwell, 2004).

4 Callum G. Brown, *The Death of Christian Britain* (London: Routledge, 2001), p. 145-69.

5 Peter L. Berger, *The Sacred Canopy* (New York: Anchor, 1969), p. 105-25.

6 In 2004 the BBC commissioned ICM Research to conduct a survey on religious belief in ten countries, *What the World Thinks of God*. Results suggest high levels of belief throughout most of the countries surveyed but only moderate levels in the UK. See BBC News (www.bbc.co.uk), "UK among most secular nations," February 26, 2004.

7 For example, the BBC survey *What the World Thinks of God* (cited above) found a higher rate of prayer than belief in the UK.

8 William James described types of faith at the turn of the last century in his influential book, *The Varieties of Religious Experience* (New York: Longmans, Green, 1902).

9   Huston Smith argues that the loss of metaphysics in contemporary
    society has been accompanied by the rise of the scientific
    worldview. See his *Why Religion Matters: the fate of the human spirit
    in an age of disbelief* (New York: HarperCollins, 2001).

10 For an account that offers insight into Galileo's day-to-day
    concerns and the complexity of his religious views, see
    Dava Sobel, *Galileo's Daughter* (Toronto: Viking, 1999).

THE QUEST FOR SECULAR JUSTICE

Our Dual Culture

I N OUR LIVES, two major forces dominate how we think about what we ought to do and how we ought to behave. One is our religious culture, which comes to us through formal and established religion as well as the broader Christian culture in which we live. The other is the structure of justice in our society. Here I would include not only our laws, courts and police, but also the community standards which, for the most part, remain unarticulated in our society.

The moral is necessarily social; it is our approach to how we interact with others – but on an eternal plane, on an outlook of forever. For Christianity, moral orientation necessarily includes the collective good, with each member of the collective taken as a person with eternal aspirations. Christianity, like the other major world religions, has this collectivism in common with communism. But communism differs from a religious moral orientation in that there is no accounting for the persistence of that aspect of human nature and creation which is fallen; indeed communism proposes a solution to the fallen world in the guise of a perfected humanist society. Western society for the most part continues to live in a dual world: with Christian and other religious cultures constantly the critics of secular society, and with a secular culture that presumes that with time, rationality, advancement, and progress, it can, if not perfect, then significantly improve the world and mankind, and thereby render religious culture obsolete.

Ethics as an articulated theory of moral behaviour is the domain of theologians and philosophers. Generally, these theories are approached by positing certain prime principles which form a starting point for codes of behaviour. In the West, these theories have a long history, dating back to classical Greek philosophers whose ideas remain highly influential. Many theories of ethics, also known as moral philosophy, have been influenced by Christianity. Some of these theories, such as that of John Rawls, articulated in *A Theory of Justice,* have attempted to understand or uncover what moral principles might be natural to human nature.

In the West, the advocacy of codes of behaviour, or the practical application of these theories to how we should behave, has been largely left to religions. Religious codes of behaviour have influenced Western society as a whole to a considerable extent. Mostly, though, they have influenced those individuals who operate in a religious milieu, or who have chosen to access them. But individuals and religious cultures do not exist in a vacuum. To get a complete understanding of what influences people's thinking on what they ought and ought not to do, we have to look at secular culture.

Right and Wrong in Secular Culture

THE CHARACTER OF right and wrong within secular society has at best been a nebulous one. Extreme theorists of secularism would argue that value impositions such as right and wrong are the holdovers from religious cultures that contemporary society must outgrow. For the most part, however, secular society continues to function with various understandings of right and wrong, however difficult they may be to define, or explain. Even those of us who feel strongly that there is no absolute "right" or "wrong" way still operate with some practical principles in our lives about what we ought to do, or will do, for the sake of good relations with other people.

All of us (I've yet to meet an exception) work with these moral forces, mixing them, weighing one against the other on points of personal preference. Within our understanding of secular justice, or a chosen religious system, we disregard certain precepts or beliefs, indefinitely or perhaps for a period in our lives. For some of us, this may be a casual juggling of moral standards as the occasion may suit, but for most, it is a heart-wrenching process by which we come to terms with that bundle of principles which we hold as true (or feel we should live up to). Sometimes, we cannot seem to reconcile all the truths and moral obligations we aspire to maintain, drawn as they are from a variety of sources. In some instances, we simply feel compelled to reject certain precepts or standards, while holding on to the rest.

Ideally, it is the moral principles of a society which ought to shape institutions that affect ethical behaviour. But articulated moral principles, or theories of justice within secular society, always seem to be in flux: in a mode of healthy debate and subject to revision. Constitutions, Bills of Rights, protection of the freedoms of individuals, laws that enshrine the rights of minorities: all these, taken together, should, in theory, be able to embody an understanding of the principles which govern action, and consequently offer us some indication of right and wrong in everyday behaviour. In practice, however, these principles provide little practical guidance for life. We routinely hear opposing sides in an ethical debate both appeal to a Bill of Rights or other enshrined principle, only to come to diametrically opposed conclusions.

Nevertheless, an understanding of right and wrong is a fundamental requirement for most people. In secular society, this comes to us through two principal means: the first is the justice system and all it entails, laws, courts, policing, etc.; the second is community standards.

System of Justice

AS A SOCIETY, we interact with our justice system at a higher level than merely that of the imposition of law and order. We interact at a theoretical level: extracting moral principles from laws, whether or not they were ever intended for this purpose. For example, the sale of illegal drugs, or more particularly the sale of illegal drugs to minors, from being a proscription in law, becomes an imperative moral prohibition for society. It is not just something that a person cannot do without suffering a consequence; the sense of its wrongfulness becomes a principle which guides society in a whole range of activities associated with the sale of dangerous products and influence over minors. Consequently, we all pass moral censure on those caught carrying out such activities or even anyone we suspect or imagine might engage in them.

The courts also have a large part to play in our understanding of right and wrong through their judgments, particularly concerning the interpretation of laws. This gets at a tricky aspect of right and wrong, where we find a conflict or feel that a person's actions, although illegal, are justified; for example, when a farmer breaks the law by growing patented seed because he feels that law, in the long term, will destroy a way of life for himself and others like him.

Policing also has a strong influence on our sense of right and wrong, where certain laws can be sometimes more, or sometimes less, stringently enforced by the police in their attempt to contain behaviour rather than dictate how people behave. Consequently, we all understand that to drive moderately over the speed limit is not wrong, but to exceed an accepted range is reprehensible, because it puts other people's lives at risk. Nevertheless, in both cases the law is being flouted.

Community Standards

THE OTHER MAJOR area within secular society affecting an understanding of right and wrong comes from what we call community standards: essentially, what is currently acceptable behaviour in the community at large. Community standards generally take over where the justice system leaves off. They tend to fluctuate over relatively short periods of time. The most precarious thing about their nature is that they tend to be unduly influenced by the politically correct. That is, they respond to emerging attitudes within our society as to which direction society ought to move in order to promote a just cause.

Community standards are volatile, and I would say dangerously so, largely because they tend to reach into areas where no accepted societal principle exists. One sometimes hears a judge appeal to community standards when the rights of an individual are either curtailed or extended. The other particularly unsettling aspect of community standards is that no one conducts an inventory of them, unlike laws or judgements, which are collected, reviewed, and able to be refined as principles that may, in turn,

71

inform the justice system. With community standards, there is little or no discussion of what society at large accepts or does not accept at a given time and of how these so-called standards relate to principles that may be enshrined in a Constitution or a Bill of Rights, or Law. There is little or no discussion of how community standards might fit into a larger structure or framework for a cohesive understanding of what society accepts. Despite their nebulous origins, community standards, or what is acceptable, the notion of "what other people do," is, I believe, second only to the justice system in influencing the understanding of right and wrong behaviour in secular society.

Secular Culture, Democracy and a Just Society

AN ATTITUDE PREVALENT today is that systems of secular justice can lead to fair societies. Despite some variety within the justice systems of secular democracies in the Western world, they are similar in a number of fundamental ways. One is that these justice systems are children of democratic societies. By maintaining a political framework in which multiple opinions are expressed and debated openly, proponents of secular justice systems believe that those elements of society that are under-represented will have their voices heard through the democratic process. This will eventually lead to fair treatment of most, if not all, sectors of society. In this framework, minorities will be appropriately represented. Another point of common understanding is that Western justice systems, though imperfect, can work together as a set of principles to form a general theory of justice which can be more than simply the sum of its parts fighting for representation from within.

Secular justice, as described above, stands in opposition to a religious understanding of what is just. There remains a dis-agreement between those who hold that democratic political systems will progress toward relatively just societies and those who maintain that an aspect of human nature is compromised through a fallen creation and thereby understand that justice itself is not achievable on the human plane. A lesson we all learn from experience is that when we demand what is good and right for us, this often leads to our demanding of those around us that they compromise on what is good and right for them. If we are to promote the well-being of those around us, we have to be prepared, when necessary, to suffer a degree of self-privation. So we see that those who maintain an under-standing of the fallen world also hold the associated religious understanding that the demand for what is just and right, or for what is owed by right to a person, as designated by a secular justice system, will always stand in opposition to the principle of non-harm of other human beings.

Moral Decisions and the Law

I HAVE OFTEN puzzled over the success of the musical *Les Misérables*. Perhaps much of its popularity was due to the song-writing and theatrical production, yet the story remains a strong indictment of secular culture. The opening scenes from the book resonated with its 19th century French audience. Here was an open condemnation on the part of Victor Hugo of the secularizing push of contemporary Republicanism and the ascendancy of secular law in that society. To the French of the time, much was made of the fact that under medieval canon, or Church law, it was not a sin for a hungry man to steal bread for his family. This Church law had a significant influence on state law in France until the time of the Revolution at the end of the 18th century. While much of the world regarded the French Revolution as a harbinger of a new era of equality and justice, the French still puzzled over the fact that secular society and secular law could not devise a system in which someone in true need was not guilty of a legal transgression.

In Hugo's novel, as in the musical, the character Jean Valjean is an embodiment of this principle and of the conundrum of secular society. Here was a man good and compassionate in deed and yet guilty in law. I do believe the audiences of *Les Misérables* sense this dichotomy. We live with the regret that no matter how hard lawmakers try, the limitations of secular law will never be able to clearly chart a path to ethical behaviour. As a society, we will always have to fall back on compassion, on a preferential treatment of the other in need, to bring about a workable peace in both our interpersonal relationships and on the higher level of international conflict.

Why Moral Decisions are Difficult

MORAL DECISIONS ARE difficult for two main reasons: one is that morality is based on principles which may contradict one another, and which people may interpret differently; and the second is that a moral decision involves an act of judgement; it involves the assertion of a value, the placing of worth on something. Despite the difficulty, we make moral decisions all the time about the value of our work, and the behaviour of our friends, family and colleagues.

Some years ago I was involved in an exercise of the Ontario government to come up with a framework for determining which issues the government was facing were environmentally significant. The government of the day had decided there had to be greater accountability on its part around environmental issues, and that the public ought to be given a means of scrutinizing government positions that could have a long-term impact on the environment. Once the government had established the general principles of the legislation, they left it to the bureaucracy to figure out which governmental decisions would be labelled significant and therefore open to public scrutiny. When the first issues came forward for potential designation as significant, a sense of panic struck the higher ranks of the civil service. No senior bureaucrat wanted to attach their name to a designation of environmental significance that would open the door to public criticism and potentially force the government to change or revise its plans.

High-ranking officials thought: *Why be associated with a potentially unpopular recommendation when surely some mechanism could be found for determining environmental significance?* So I was asked to be part of a panel that would tame this mysterious beast, environmental significance: an easy task, or so we thought. We quickly drew up several expanded definitions of the concept of environmental significance. But the frustrations of senior bureaucrats remained, when they set these definitions against the growing mound of decisions and projects coming forward that needed either to be designated as having, or be cleared of having, environmental significance. They had no problem applying the definition to a request to build an oil refinery next to a large urban development. In the majority of cases, however, the definitions were of no help. They could not help in deciding on the environmental significance of a request for a permit to extract an additional 15 metric tons of ground water in an agricultural area, nor in deciding on a request for rezoning from commercial to light industrial near a waterway.

75

So we were asked to go back to the drawing board.

It became clear that what senior bureaucrats wanted was some sort of magic box. They wanted a receptacle into which one could dump the environmental principles the government had adopted, along with a plethora of detailed environmental standards, such as acceptable emission rates for chemicals in the air. Then, one by one, individual government decisions, however routine, could be thrown into the mix, and, after giving the box a good shake, out would come the answer to whether or not the decision was environmentally significant.

My fellow panel members and I responded with a fully interactive tick-off-the-box form: "Does this decision affect the government's long term strategy for environmental sustainability? Does this decision affect the government's long term plans to maintain the current level of biodiversity in the province?" Once the high-level principles were dealt with, the form moved on to accepted standards, in page after page of: "Does this decision affect land? Surface water? Aquifer? Emissions? Known contaminants? Toxins?" etc.

We went through the exercise, producing what was expected, only to come to the same conclusion. At the end of the form was one more box: "Therefore this decision is environmentally significant: Yes or No?" Regardless of how it was broken down, whatever issues went into the mix, there was no avoiding the inevitable: someone would have to sign their name to a document that assigned value. Someone would have to make a judgement.

Judgement

AS HUMAN BEINGS we have an extreme aversion to making judgements, knowingly placing value on things. We want to know what is right, not decide what is right. *What is a good bottle of wine? Who are the great artists?* Deciding on what is right and wrong is no different. Moral decisions are difficult.

Every assignment of moral value is participation – conscious participation – in an imperfect world. The processes we go through in our personal lives are much the same as the exercise of determining environmental significance. They are even quite similar to making judgements of aesthetic value when we like things. We are going through a process of placing value when we think things are good for the health of the world, and when we think personal or social behaviour is good for society or even for ourselves and our personal integrity. In many ways, this seems like a process of recognizing value, value which is already there and only needs clarity of mind to be discerned. Whether or not the value is intrinsically there is a debate we can leave to the philosophers. Whether it is there or not, recognizing value is tantamount to passing judgement.

Nazi atrocities or war crimes in the former Yugoslavia, and other issues like these, become clearer when we go through the process of examining the fundamental principles to which we adhere. When we consider which principles apply, and the practical circumstances of law and community standards that are at play in a particular case, when we go through a lengthy process like this, the value we arrive at in the end sometimes seems like a non-issue. It may appear as though we have established the value through the process, and that the outcome is inevitable once we have examined the issues.

Because it is the contentious moral issues that are debated

77

and cause real divisions in our society, the overall impression left is of a society in moral conflict. I suggest that just the reverse is true. In the course of a day, a human being makes a large number of moral judgements, judgements that pass for opinions or mere thoughts. In reality, the big issues are a small proportion of the moral issues we address. On a daily basis, we pass judgement on the behaviour of our colleagues, spouses and children, and on our political leaders for their decisions or their lack of action or courage. We make moral judgements when we say the driver passing too quickly down a residential street is doing something wrong, regardless of whatever tension, anxiety, or stress the driver may feel. We make these kinds of judgements without thinking, and we make so many of them that we live in a pool of value, a fairly harmonious pool despite irritants and disagreement on some issues.

When we make moral judgements unreflectively, it comes quite easily to us. But strangely, as soon as we move into the realm of self-awareness of moral decisions, we become reluctant to pass judgement on hot issues, like abortion, same sex marriage, reproductive rights, military spending, support for allies, conflicts in the Middle East, or intervention in countries by third parties. On all these issues, we struggle with the fundamental principles on which we might base moral decisions. *What do we believe on the issue of the primacy of life? The absolute protection of the innocent?* We struggle with how these fundamental principles can be applied in particular situations, with what legislative regimes, types of law, and systems of law might or should pertain, and with issues of who has authority to act and in what areas. We also struggle with the reasoning we apply to how fundamental principles interact with their specific application. We struggle with our final assessment of making a decision on where our reason should lead us. Ultimately, we struggle with the passing of judgement, with the laying on of value, and with the moral conclusions to which our reason has led us.

The Cycle of Renewal

BEING A STUDENT of comparative religion, I have seen people come to the field, particularly those specializing in the Eastern religions, by way of a personal rejection of the West and its religious traditions. For someone in the West, either religious or secular, the religions of the East can be inspiring because of their emphasis on enlightenment, their rich cultural heritage, and the breadth of their diversity. To someone from the West looking at these religions through the lens of Western culture, the conditions of not being born to a higher caste or the overbearing entrapment of desire do not cut nearly so deeply as they do for someone from the East.

As I studied the religions of the Eastern world and began to see these traditions as complex societal structures, some of the lessons of comparative religion were brought home to me. The first of these was the similarity of religions East and West in promoting negative incentives for change.

This struck me in a startlingly simple way when listening to the lyrics of a song by Joni Mitchell: "Guru books, the Bible, only a reminder that you're just not good enough." The songs of Joni Mitchell represent for me what the 1960s meant to a generation of North Americans. And though the hope of that generation appears to be largely lost, personally I feel as though I salvaged one ugly truth: that the function of religion in society is largely a negative one.

Every religion has a cycle of recognizing value in moral behaviour, of passing judgement on behaviour, and of demanding

79

that people take responsibility for their actions when they operate within this sphere of value and judgement. From a theoretical point of view, it seems like a system in which, if you abide by the rules, you can stay out of trouble. Yet, in every religious system I know, it is impossible to live up to such ideals. The cycle of value, judgement and responsibility necessarily leaves everyone falling short.

I have described this cycle in particularly Western and Christian terms, yet I do believe that the fundamental issues hold true for all major religions. Equally true is that they all offer a way out, through models such as those of rebirth and enlightenment in the East, or of law, obedience and sacrifice in the West. Some form of recognition that we are lacking, and the action of offering a sacrifice, asking for forgiveness and acknowledgement of sin – these provide a vehicle for renewal that takes us back into the cycle toward some form of final release. These cycles are found in every major religion. Similarly, they are found in the traditional religions of Africa, Asia, and North and South America, many of which centre on cults of sacrificial offering, penance and renewal.

Secular Society and the Cycle of Renewal

A RELIGIOUS WORLDVIEW maintains that the goal of secular society, to create a relatively just society, is fundamentally unattainable. It asserts that the only alternative is a stance of compassion. This view will always be seen as being soft where a stick is needed, with regard to the application of the law, courts, legal action, and preventing individuals from harming others. But universal justice is hardly limited to the imposition of universal laws to prevent crime and misdemeanours. A just society would be one in which all human beings are allowed to develop appropriately to their own situations, with their own families, peoples and cultures, toward a sense of their own fulfilment and the realization of their livelihood.

Western secular culture has no means of placing issues of the scope of the economic hegemony of the West over the rest of world within the cycle of value, judgement, responsibility and renewal. Secular justice has no means of insuring justice for those whose self-determination is withheld, particularly those in the developing world. Secular justice, furthermore, has to assume that those in the Western world who are the instruments (and we are all collectively the instruments) of economic hegemony are acting after a just fashion.

Secular society is not completely divorced from the realities of the cycle of renewal. Some, if not all, secularists accept that we function in a value-laden structure. Secular society also accepts judgement as being a logical consequence of value. It sees the need for placing judgement, and even builds structures to assign judgement. These can be legal institutions or frameworks which embody the law, such as the rules of the road, or might be the precepts of international law employed by the International Criminal Tribunal in The Hague. They might also be such things as cultural institutions which give voice to public opinion: for example, environmental critics or editorial pages.

At the point of responsibility, however, secular society attempts to break with the cycle of renewal. Here secular society and its justice structures can accept and assign responsibility to individuals for individual actions, but there is only begrudging and limited acknowledgement of universal responsibility, whereby each of us participates in social structures larger than ourselves and on the part of which we must accept responsibility for the harm they may cause. Each of us individually and collectively creates value, makes judgements and is responsible. Here secular society is attempting to opt out of the cycle, rather than following through with the next step of recognition of responsibility and renewal. Guilt becomes the consequence of not following through on the acknowledgement of responsibility and ensuing mechanisms of renewal (recognition of sin, transgression or failure and seeking forgiveness and reconciliation).

Secular society takes an opposing position. It believes that it is slowly effecting a universal change through its imposition of judgement and limited responsibility for individual acts, and that, given the opportunity, it would be able to implement a relatively just society, not only for Western nations, but for the entire world, through the promotion of education, law, democracy and well-being. Despite the benefits of this approach, individual and collective feelings of guilt and unresolved acknowledgement of responsibility have profound repercussions for secular society.

The Response of Secular Culture to the Cycle of Renewal

SECULAR CULTURE responds to the cycle on three levels. The first is through adopting a stance of progressive secularization, such as that in the theory of secularization which I described in the previous chapter. Here the expectation is that a final sense of resolution to the cycle will be brought about by the eradication of religion, which secular society sees as the author of the cycle.

On a second level, secular culture carries on a "dialogue of the extremes" in order to set the boundaries of right and wrong and determine moral orientation. It throws together both religious and secular influences, sometimes as a confused jumble, sometimes as a semi-orderly dialogue. At one and the same time, an understanding of the "way to act" is influenced by the austerity of the Puritans, the spirituality of medieval monasticism, or the Southern Baptist Convention's condemnation of the lack of family values in the "new" Disney.

In what passes for a morbid curiosity about religious moral standards or punishments, secular society draws a fringe around moral behaviour, and, just outside of this fringe, it isolates for censure a certain level of what it views as extreme, outlandish, or unreasonable conduct. In Northern Ontario, where I grew up, and where to be French-Canadian was to be a second-class citizen, this fringe was often associated with the practices of Catholicism. Through the fringe floated strange notions of bodily deprivation through fasting during Lent, or that a priest could dictate one's future behaviour through assigning a penance. As social structures have changed in Ontario and North America, and following the changes of the Second Vatican Council, Catholicism and its practices ceased to fulfil that unwitting role in the dialogue of the extremes. Society then looked to religious practices in marginalized fundamentalist Christian groups or other religions in order to populate the fringe. In particular, Islam has entered into the dialogue, and one now hears things such as: "If you are a Muslim, you can have your hand cut off for robbery." The accuracy of such comments, in which countries they might be true under which circumstances, and in what decade or century, all seem to become irrelevant. The real issue is that in secular society there exists an imaginative space needing to be filled by the intimation that there is consequence for immoral behaviour. Secular society can reject the authority of a religious system to say what our behaviour should be by placing that religious system outside the fringe of the reasonable. At the same time, this fringe allows secular culture to design its own matrix of acceptable and unacceptable behaviours, and decide which lie on the fringe, and which are within the realm of the acceptable.

The Root of All Ills

ON A THIRD level, secular culture responds to the cycle of renewal by designating religion as the root of all ills. This was brought home to me a number of years ago, when the publisher Penguin Canada arranged a public forum on ethics. Several writers presented big-picture ideas on the state of morality and invited members of the audience to respond. As is typical of such public debates, the discourse remained in the arena of secular understanding of morality and rationalist philosophy. Christian perspectives or broader religious understandings of morality were carefully capped, but lurking under the surface; and remained there until one presenter, a medical doctor, suggested in a humorous, yet pointed way that religion was the cause of society's ills, and had been throughout history. Only its eradication, he suggested, would lead to a better society. The audience was highly entertained.

In the question period, I was surprised to see Katherine Young step forward. As one of Canada's pre-eminent scholars of comparative religion, she is internationally known for her work on Eastern feminist cultures. She challenged our humorous presenter by suggesting that his depiction of religion as the cause of the world's ills and strife was patently absurd. In response, he belittled her as though she were a Christian fundamentalist, to the great delight of the audience.

I found myself in the twilight zone. Before me was a scholar

who had spent a lifetime publishing on Eastern religious traditions, who could be highly critical of the West and its moral
assumptions, and who presented a strong feminist critique of
interpretations of religions both East and West. I was watching
her being ridiculed by a popular writer to the great satisfaction
of thousands of well-educated, jeering people.

This reminded me of an experience of my own several years
before, when I was irritated by a radio commentator's attack
on religion as the cause of war in Northern Ireland. I took to
my desk in a twenty-four hour writing frenzy, where I
sketched out what I saw as the self-evident arguments to prove
the contrary. Not a single case of civil strife can be found in
the world today in which one side of the conflict is not significantly economically disadvantaged. Throughout history, and
I assert this emphatically, there is not one exception to this
rule. Civil strife is fundamentally economic. Groups in conflict use religious and ethno-cultural distinctions to assert
economic hegemony. When ethno-cultural/religious groups
are taken out of their indigenous situation — as was the case
with Catholics and Protestants from Northern Ireland who
exported their conflicts to Toronto and New England — conflict
persists only until relative economic parity is achieved.
Christian and Arab groups around the Mediterranean basin
have had similar experiences. History offers no instance of
war or dissention between ethno-cultural/religious groups
without economic disparity, or an attempt to assert political
authority in a bid to gain economic control.

After spending a day churning out my arguments, I recall
heading to the library in search of references. I found there,
huddled on a shelf next to each other, half a dozen crisp
unused books all with variations on the title *Does Religion Cause
War?* Reviewing the table of contents of each, I found all my

arguments charted out in a similar manner. It struck me that no one had read these books and that no one would read mine.

The role the Spanish Inquisition has come to play in popular discourse offers a similar lesson. The historical fact of the Spanish Inquisition is one of the most enduring and generally applied objections to religion in Western society. This argument might be used against someone espousing the merits of religious education, or against the mainline churches' uncompromising opposition to war. Although the Spanish Inquisition took place in a different century and was the product of a particular faction within the Church and its co-option by the Spanish imperial forces, nevertheless, the objection that the Spanish Inquisition existed is applied with considerable success in expressing opposition to the moral, spiritual, or practical undertakings of any or all Christian Churches. We are so accustomed to hearing and accepting the legitimacy of this blanket objection that just about any response to it is ineffectual. The practically-minded, those seeking an emotional response, and even hard-nosed fact-dependent academics, all accept the objection of the Spanish Inquisition.

It may help to try to step aside and see what it is we are giving credence to when we entertain this argument. What would a similar argument look like in politics? We might choose the persecution of Thomas-à-Becket for his views on the rights of kings. Would this then mean that we could look to the twelfth century, to a political system different from ours, in order to draw conclusions about whether we should accept decisions of the state in Canada in the twenty-first century? If someone were to propose that Canada's anti-terrorism laws needed strengthening in order to preserve democracy, could we respond with: What about the persecution of Thomas-à-Becket?

Would we dismiss the health system when it advises the public to lead a healthier lifestyle by objecting that, for centuries, physicians let blood? We do not entertain this type of reasoning in any field except religion. Why is this? The reason lies partly in the motivations of religious groups themselves, and springs from, not only their willingness, but their conviction, to see history as a totality; it is, in a way, a taking of responsibility for the sins of one's ancestors. Apologies for actions may well come after the death of participants. But there should be some continuity of moral, political and economic motivations, along with the practices of the repentant organization. Nevertheless, when it comes to history, the Churches see themselves as apart from other institutions; they desire to view themselves as part of eternal history.

Secular culture does not want to hear about the Churches' understanding of their mission to history, just as it does not want to hear that religion does not cause war, because the issue at play is not that the Churches continue to commit the errors of centuries past, but rather the deep-seated need of secular culture to blame religion for being the cause of society's ills. By laying responsibility at the doorstep of the Churches, secular culture attempts to discredit the methods of resolution to the cycle of renewal offered by religion. Religious culture, by contrast, invites everyone to participate in the cycle and believes this will lead, even if only partially, to what society as a whole is searching for in secular justice: the sense of resolution that a final justice might offer.

A Religious and Secular Culture

WE LIVE IN a dual culture. In our society, some people claim to hold to a religious view and others claim to hold to a secular view, when, in reality, it is difficult for anyone to escape being influenced by both religious and secular ideas. In the

West, our views on ethics are influenced by the religious culture in terms of traditional Christian teaching on morality;
while secular culture influences us through secular ideas of
right and wrong and community standards.

Secular culture is attempting to achieve a just society, though
it is frustrated by its inability to achieve its ideals. Religious culture also works hard for the betterment of society but believes
that a perfectly just society is fundamentally impossible and
makes a response of compassion. Religious society sees itself as
being in a cycle of value, judgement, responsibility and reconciliation. Secular society can see responsibility and guilt, but has no
mechanism to incorporate reconciliation into its worldview. It
also has difficulty dealing with collective responsibility. Secular
culture responds by blaming religion and takes the position that
the eradication of religion will bring about its desired goals.
Religion, on the other hand, believes that only a response of
compassion to others, which can lead to forgiveness and renewal
and bring people into the cycle, will lead to any sense of final
resolution.

CONCLUSION

TOWARDS THE END of the Cold War, when China began to open up, the first reports of visitors who were allowed to travel in the provinces began to circulate. Around that time, a professor of mine, Willard Oxtoby, was invited to give a series of lectures throughout the country. As was typical of visits to communist countries in that era, he was accompanied, day and night, both by secret service and by a group of Chinese professors of religion who were his hosts.

Days into the tour, on a long train ride through the country, when they were finally alone together, Professor Oxtoby's Chinese hosts let their guard drop and turned to him: "Now we want to ask you the real question. Why is it that evil people get ahead?"

This question says many things about religious belief and secular justice, but charged as it is, in the meeting of professors from the capitalist and communist worlds, its meaning seems almost infinite. It should be remembered that in doctrinaire communist countries of the time, religion was the subject of academic research for one reason: which was to facilitate its demise.

The question and the manner in which these communist scholars asked it was revealing in several ways: it suggested they had discussed this problem secretly amongst themselves; it suggested they thought a scholar from the West, if he did not have the answer, might have some insights for them; it suggested that, though they were the experts in the attempts of a secular culture to achieve a final sense of justice, they had seemingly concluded that a secular communism did not have the answer; and the reference to "evil people" acknowledged a value system a visitor from the West could immediately comprehend.

I think that, in a way, we are all one of the Chinese scholars on the train. We are asking the same questions about religious and secular cultures. We understand that the world's major religions are concerned with making their environments a better place, but more importantly, that they are concerned with the ultimate ends of people, their final salvation, or liberation, and that this relates to the fulfilment of a relationship with the transcendent.

At the same time, like these scholars, we not only operate in, but identify with, a secular culture. We acknowledge that these secular cultures are also concerned with creating a better world, whether they be a communist culture focused on equality and material wellbeing, or Western-style democratic cultures, which promote a controlled competitive environment to bring about material wellbeing while supporting social structures for the promotion of a just society. Like these scholars, we are faced with the emotional and intellectual conundrum that there is a fundamental non-fit in our daily lives between the just and fair society we think human beings have the potential to create and the injustice of social relations that we experience. And like the Chinese scholars perplexed at why evil people are getting ahead, we are capable of looking to both religious cultures and secular cultures for answers.

Turning back to the questions people have asked me over the years about religion, I would like to respond by drawing three conclusions from each of my chapters. I would hope that these three conclusions would form a partial answer to the question the Chinese scholars posed on the train; a question which is, I think, one form of the fundamental questions we are all asking about our dual culture and the possibility of a just society.

The first conclusion concerns the personage of the historical figure of Jesus of Nazareth. Why are we perpetually fascinated with discovering the details of his personal life when there is very little that can be known from the available sources? Why is it that over the past one hundred and fifty years, scholars have been asserting the humanity of Jesus, over his divinity, to great popular acclaim, only to have this phenomenon repeat again and again? As with this and other questions about the historical figure of Jesus I raised in the first chapter, I would draw the conclusion that we as a society are continually trying to know the transcendent personality, and that we can to a degree know this personality through certain transcendent-temporal junctures, which in the West we call the sacramental. All the world's major faiths have mechanisms for "knowing the transcendent" which parallel the sacramental. In the West, this knowing is embodied in the figure of Jesus.

The second conclusion I would draw, again implicit in the Chinese scholars' question, is that religion is not going away. Figures on belief and religious practice demonstrate that religious adherence has not fundamentally changed over the past two hundred years, that fluctuations are normal, and that perceptions of a past "age of faith" are a historical projection not based on fact. Like the Chinese scholars, we find we are not in a paradigm of faith versus loss-of-faith, or of faith versus atheism; rather, we are critically questioning faith and can continue to do so without falling into one of the prescribed modes.

The last conclusion I would draw is that, in a way, our views of the potential for a just society are similar to those of the

JESUS AND THE QUEST FOR SECULAR JUSTICE

Chinese scholars. For the most part, these scholars would have been educated in a post-revolutionary communist environment, in which atheism was the official position of the educational system; yet, it would seem, they doubted the ability of a secular state to bring about a just society.

Religions, like secular cultures, recognize that there is value in social relations; that we are ethical beings; and that people need to acknowledge responsibility for their actions. Yet religious cultures offer a way out through their understanding of cycles of renewal: value, judgement, responsibility, and reconciliation. Secular cultures have so far failed in their attempts to create just societies; and in so far as they attempt to opt out of the cycle of renewal at the point of responsibility, they are bound to blame religion for being the cause of unresolved acknowledgement of responsibility. Religious cultures stand aside from secular cultures, invite people into a process of renewal, and point toward the final end of their own liberation and fulfilment.

About the Author

Pierre L'Abbé holds a Ph.D. in Comparative Religion from the University of Toronto. He has taught world religions and ethics at the University of Toronto and Humber College. Religion and morality in contemporary society are major themes in his poetic works, *Lyon* (Letters, 1996) and *Ten Days in Rio* (watershedBooks, 1998). His concerns on the interplay of aesthetics, morality, and religion come together in critical writings art in southeast Asia and politics in Europe, and in his short story collection, *In the Time of Talking* (Guernica Editions, 2005).